SURRENDER AT ROCKY POINT

Table of Contents

Slabtown

Sixth grade lunchtime was such a memorable time. I sat with my friends, Debbie and Sharon. The three of us were at an age where we had become interested in boys and particularly the upperclassman (7th graders). On many occasions, we pretended to be listening to the teacher while writing notes and secretly passing them to one another. I recall most of our notes contained career dreams and hopes of a bright future, dreams of an upscale apartment in the city, living a life of independence and, of course, with lots of money. We managed to make good grades, but we were incredibly sneaky in our efforts to communicate while the teacher gave instruction. Our dreams could not be contained. We inked up the wide-ruled notebook paper with our ideas of what life would be like after graduation. We passed the notes back and forth during class being very careful to go unnoticed.

When the lunch bell sounded, we rushed to the cafeteria. We anxiously awaited lunchtime each day. We were able to mingle with the 7th grade students. During this time Debbie had grown fond of a boy who we called Davy. Davy was named after his uncle, David Lee Scott, who was killed in Vietnam in April of 1968. His body was never recovered. David's father, Bob, called him "Davy".

My devotion was never focused on any boy for very long, maybe two to three weeks at the longest, but Debbie was different. Her loyalty and her admirations seemed very attentive. Davy appeared to feel the same about Debbie. They looked for every opportunity to spend time together in between classes and at break time.

We had fun in each class, but we particularly looked forward to our afternoon class, typewriting. I recall Debbie and her beautiful long skinny fingers and her long, always healthy manicured fingernails as they typed. She was packed full of talent. One could not help but admire her gifts. She played the piano, was a basketball team manager, was confident in her public speaking, and was stocked full of etiquette and class. Debbie was attentive to achieving goals to further herself in college and in her future career.

I remember the clunking of the manual typewriter keys striking the paper as we practiced our typing skills. "Now is the time for all good men to come to the aid of their country". We typed this sentence over and over as we practiced our timed typing skills. I think I typed it in my sleep! If I was sitting idle for any length of time, I was moving my fingers with the same keystrokes, "Now is the time for all good men to come to the aid of their country."

I dreamed of attending college, but never believed it would become a reality. My only hope was to earn scholarships to pay my way. Reluctantly, I tried not to focus on college excessively for fear I would not be able to afford to attend.

I attended the Symsonia Elementary & High School until 1985 when the entire county of Graves consolidated seven small schools into one large high school located in Mayfield, Kentucky.

The mere thought of attending a large school with seven other schools gave someone like me extreme anxiety. I found it very challenging to form new friendships because I was not outgoing. Debbie, on the other hand, was fearless to forging new friendships and learning new faces. It seemed as if Debbie had never met a stranger. Her introductions were always graceful yet confident. I was continuously in awe of the way she lit up the room upon her entry. She had a way of bringing brightness and joy to a room. There was a light inside of her which magnetically attracted people.

Just as I imagined, settling into the new high school was not easy. The school was huge compared to our small community school of Symsonia. I found myself yearning for a familiar face. I hoped I would get to see at least one of my old Symsonia friends. Those occasions were rare. That small school of Symsonia was now scattered like grains of sand amid seven other schools. I only had a few classes with some of my old acquaintances and was painfully forced to form new relationships.

I met Debbie and Sharon in the main commons area of the school before the first bell rang. Later, Debbie and Davy broke up but continued as friends. I recall discreetly rolling our eyes in disgust and giggling uncontrollably when we saw Davy with other girls. It was hard to imagine

Davy with anyone else but Debbie. They were meant to be together forever! Their chemistry was obvious to me.

My heart ached for the close bond we shared in the small country school in the small community of Symsonia, otherwise known as "Slabtown". The legendary story was this: Symsonia received the nickname "Slabtown" because cars drove on wooden slabs in the early days before roads were constructed. I had left my heart in Symsonia and this new school was a huge shock for a shy, awkward, teenage girl to seek survival. I wore my self-esteem issues like a 50-pound feed sack on my shoulders. Agonizingly, I found a few new friends my sophomore year. Finally, by my junior year, I was able to share a few classes with Debbie again.

Homecoming Queen

It was my senior year of high school and the weekend of Thanksgiving 1987. My sister and I were on our way to Paducah to purchase a bicycle for her kids, a 25-mile journey from my home in Hickory. The nearest town, Mayfield, was a very small town with few retail outlets. As we made our trip on Highway 131, I noticed a Kentucky State Police car stopped at the top of the hill speaking to a boy named Jason. Something caught my eye causing to me to look to the right side of the road and there I saw Debbie's smashed and mangled car in the woods. I was very familiar with the location because it was a wooded area close to my typing teacher's house. I stopped to ask Jason if Debbie was okay. He explained an ambulance had transported her to the Lourdes Hospital. I immediately left his driveway and drove straight to the hospital. As soon as I entered the waiting area, I could sense the severity of the situation. Things were intense, and I could feel the dark heaviness in the room. I quickly realized my friend Debbie was in trouble. The room began to fill with people as word spread. I felt so weak in my knees I remember sliding down the wall and sitting on the floor. More and more students learned of the accident and began to file into the hospital one by one. Debbie's parents allowed us to enter her hospital room at scheduled times to see her. The picture of Debbie lying in the hospital bed is engraved in my mind. She was all hooked up to machines and tubes. My friend was in an unresponsive coma. How could this be?

I reluctantly returned to school though my mind was fixed on Debbie. The staff and our principal made every effort to allow us time to comfort one another. We found comfort by telling old stories of our Symsonia "Slabtown" days.

I will never forget the dim afternoon on Wednesday, December 2, 1987. I was sitting in my chemistry classroom. I remember Mrs. Young and Mrs. Wiggins walking into the classroom. I knew something was wrong. You could read their body language. They slowly eased into the room and made eye contact with me. Mrs. Wiggins turned on the school television for an interschool televised announcement. Our principal announced to the school Debbie had been removed from life support and had passed away. I will never forget dropping my head to my desk and crying uncontrollably. The teachers walked back to my chair and began to console me. The classroom was filled with tears and sobs.

I had found a way of mental escape for me was to journal my thoughts. I loved to write poetry and had been constructing poems since I was in the fourth grade. Because I was shy and awkward and was not comfortable speaking in a crowd, I found my liberation from the struggles and stress of home life came through writing and studying. I could express my feelings and release pressure. A pen and paper were always my faithful companion.

Debbie's parents arranged for Debbie's funeral on a Saturday at a local Symsonia church. I wrote a poem about Debbie. It was read at her funeral by my friend, Casey. He was in the same school clubs as Debbie and me. Debbie was in Future Business Leaders of America otherwise known as FBLA. She had traveled to several competitions outside of school. During her funeral, Casey shared with the congregation some unforgettable traits regarding Debbie: "She always had her Bible in her suitcase when she traveled." I will never forget those words of declaration.

Losing Debbie was my first experience with the death of a friend. I had lost an aunt when I was five years old. I remember vaguely the sadness of the house during that time, but I was much too young to remember all the specifics. This time I was old enough to experience the lingering sadness death introduced and its permanent and lasting impact. I watched her seat be empty in the classroom and it left me sad and empty on the inside.

Before her death, Debbie had been unanimously voted as Homecoming Queen. Her parents returned to our school and accepted her award. I will never forget the look of grief on her parent's face as they accepted their daughter's award. The sorrow on their face could not be overcome with a hint of a smile. There was tremendous sadness throughout the gymnasium as people rose to their feet, hands began to clap, and eyes welled with tears watching as her mom and dad accepted Debbie's award. It all seemed like a bad nightmare. On graduation night I filed past her empty seat as the band played *"Pomp & Circumstance"*.[1] I solemnly examined her empty chair draped with her graduation gown and tassels. If only she could come back! I missed her terribly!

Her laughter, her kindness, her compassion for life, the way she held herself, and the life she lived made a profound influence on me. She was a true example of grace and inner beauty. I had looked up to her as a role model since our friendship began in the sixth grade. Etched on her grey granite tombstone sitting under the shade of trees in the Clarks River Cemetery:

October 2, 1970 - December 2, 1987

For the first time in my life, I was learning what the date on the right side of the "dash" meant from a deeper more personal view. The end of the dash for my friend, Debbie: December 2nd of 1987. At the age of 17, I learned life is cruelly fragile and death is painfully final.

Davy returned from college to attend Debbie's funeral and the gatherings which followed. We began to spend time together talking. In an act of boldness, I invited him to my high school dance. Later, we began dating and became inseparable. We married in August 1989, the beginning of my sophomore year of college. Like most new couples we rushed everything to create a homestead. We rushed into getting a cat, then a dog. And like so many new married couples wonder what was next on the list! We were in a hurry for everything—rushing adulthood. We certainly had the "what's next?" mentality. And so, we believed we were ready for the next addition to our home-- a baby. I found out I was pregnant in January 1991. We were both so young and unprepared.

Davy and I had discussed numerous baby names. We settled on a girl's name but could not agree on a boy's name. We had gone to the hospital after my water broke. However, they sent me back home. I had no idea what to expect with our first baby. Later that night I returned to the hospital in hard labor. A boy's name was selected while we were on our way to the hospital. The country music song, *"Feed Jake" by Pirates of the Mississippi* [2]came on the radio as Davy was driving at a high rate of speed to the hospital in our neighboring town of Murray almost 30 miles away. Davy proclaimed "Jake" was the name and I had the perfect middle name selected. It all went together perfectly. Yes, finally, we had a name if the baby was a boy. (I admit I knew nothing about the song except the dog was named Jake. Davy loved the name!)

Jacob Ross Scott was born at 1:46 a.m. on September 29th, by natural childbirth. He was beautiful with blue eyes and a perfectly shaped head. As a new young mother, I was terrified to find out he had a touch of jaundice requiring a longer stay in the hospital. Once we were home, we parked his crib in front of a bright sunny window to help his bilirubin levels drop to normal. To us, there was no other child in all the world. He was the center of our world. When Jacob arrived, it changed me. I felt a different kind of love I had never experienced—a mother's love for her infant. The instant protective instincts came immediately with my first glance at this beautiful baby boy.

At a very young age, Jake discovered a love for the outdoors and hunting just like his father. Jake was a "hands-on" kid. He loved to take everything apart and put it back together. Everything we purchased for him had to be completely disassembled. He wasn't happy unless he was dismantling a toy. He would put it back together which was always amazing to both of us. Even as a very small child, we recognized an incredible gift Jake possessed. He was very good working with his hands.

Jake developed a love for weather just like his father. Much to our amazement, he was not terrified of storms. One evening during a bad thunderstorm, he insisted on opening the door. Because the door opened to the exterior, the storm's strong wind caught the door and launched him over the steps and into the back yard. He was fine with no scratches or bruises. This terrified Davy and me. But even this episode did not scare him of the weather. He remained inquisitive of passing storms. As a small child, he discovered his favorite movie of all times was the movie, *"Twister"* starring *Bill Paxton* and *Helen Hunt*. This movie, released on May 10, 1996, was a movie about a team of storm chasers who researched tornadoes. They bravely chased tornadoes to gather data about each tornado in order to improve warning systems.[3] Our little Jacob had the movie on an old VHS tape, and he watched it repeatedly. While other kids were obsessed with animated movies and television shows, he was preoccupied with tornadoes. As I traveled out of town on business, I often brought a gift home for Jake. On a return trip from Dallas, Texas I purchased Jake a tornado globe at an airport gift shop. It was like a snow globe except it was columnar in shape and when you shook it the glitter inside formed a twister. His eyes lit up in astonishment, "Cool. Mom, it's a tornado!" He played with it so much he wore the "Texas Tornado" letters off the model. This child was strangely fascinated with nature and weather.

There was a strained work/life balance as Davy and I both worked a lot of hours. To add to the hectic pace, Jake was involved in both football and basketball. We put lots of miles on the vehicles as we traveled to sporting events. Most of our weekends involved practices, games, sports banquets, or tournaments. We traveled every opportunity to the "away" games. Jake was excited as he collected trophies, plaques, and team pictures each season. Eventually, we purchased two solid oak bookshelves and placed them in his room so he could display his trophy collection. We were proud to look at those trophies and all he had accomplished while playing sports.

After believing I suffered from severe fatigue, we received a pleasant but unplanned surprise in 2002. When Jake was eleven years old, we informed him he was going to have a little brother. Hunter was born 3 days after Jacob's birthday on October 2nd by emergency C-section due to stroke level blood pressure resulting from toxemia.

From the moment we brought Hunter home from the hospital Jake was in love with him. He played with him constantly. It was almost as if he had a life-sized toy in Hunter. Jake enjoyed his new role as a big brother and adapted nicely. He loved teaching Hunter how to play ball and how to do all those adventurous boy things in life.

We lived in a rural country neighborhood of Hickory, KY. We were so blessed with good neighbors who had children the same ages. The children grew close as they continued playing and expanding their adventures each year. There was plenty of land with creeks and streams available to them for deeper exploration. When Jake was fifteen, after much begging and pleading, we reluctantly purchased an ATV for him. The boys loved riding ATV's. As they grew, they began to practice their mechanic skills on their ATV's. After the fascination with ATV's fizzled out, a new-found love for vehicles soon followed. Their high school ag and shop classes taught them new skills fostering a deeper appreciation for the inner mechanics of their cars and trucks. Our garage blossomed into a popular local neighborhood hangout as they practiced their trade skills and stretched their wings demonstrating increased freedom. Often, their independence sparked boyhood mischief leaving behind some minor messes for dad to clean.

Though Jake was discovering his independence, he was never embarrassed to give Davy or me a hug and plant a kiss right on the lips before he left the house. When he hugged you it's like you could feel the warmth swirling inside your soul saturating every fiber of your body with his love. He generously showered his affection on Davy, Hunter, and me. His long arms offered great hugs, too awesome for words. He had so much love for his family. As a mom I cherished the evenings he laid at the foot of my bed watching television until it was bedtime. "Mom, would you rub my back?" was his favorite pre-bedtime request.

And just like that, I blinked, and Jake was a senior in high school. I could not bring myself to get his college registration things ready. I don't know if I was experiencing the anxiety of letting him go to college, but I hesitated to register him. Maybe I just couldn't let go of him to send him to college? I found new reasons to delay. I could not tolerate the thought of him leaving. But I could tell Jake was not ready for this big step. And so, we both procrastinated all college preparations.

Jake worked a part-time job every day after school loading trucks at a local bottling distribution company. He enjoyed earning money and depositing it into his bank account. He was wise with his money. He enjoyed fixing up his truck and equipping it with new stereo equipment and speakers. He kept it maintained with all the basics. Each evening I had trouble falling asleep until I heard the loud exhaust on his white 2000 *Chevrolet Silverado* truck pulling into our driveway. I was edgy until I was soothed by the sound of his recognizable custom exhaust. When I heard that exhaust, I knew he was home and I could ease off to sleep.

In 2008, Jake added waterfowl to his list of hunting pastimes along with hunting deer and turkey. Just like prior years, the Christmas wish list reflected another hobby requiring more storage in the shop. Admittingly, I knew very little about duck hunting. It was like a foreign language to me!

Of no surprise, the Christmas of 2008, Jake was elated to open a box and find his new chest waders along with other hunting supplies selected and purchased by his father and his Aunt Chrissy.

Jake and his friends enjoyed going to area ponds and setting up their duck decoys. Because Davy was not a duck hunter, he had friends who took Jake hunting on Lake Barkley and Kentucky Lake. As Jake's passion for duck hunting grew so did his traveling radius, venturing to the neighboring state of Missouri to duck hunt.

Instinct

On January 9, 2009, after work I traveled to a local home improvement store and purchased my weekend project materials. The bathroom shared by Davy and Jake was in desperate need of an update. That evening Jake was in the shop along with his friends working on their vehicles and stereo equipment. I worked around the house then later heard Jake enter the door and make his way upstairs to his room. I walked to the living room and called his name. He answered and said, "Hey, mom! I am home. Trevor is spending the night. We are getting up early in the morning to go duck hunting. We are going to bed now because we have to get up early." I remarked, "Ok. I was just making sure you were home because I am going to bed."

The next morning, January 10, 2009, Jake and his friends loaded up and met at his friend, Mckenzie's home. Jake left his truck there and traveled with his friends to Kentucky Lake. During their trip, Jake called Davy between 4:30 to 5:00 a.m. to ask him where Highway 1422 turn-off was located. This highway leads to Little Bear Highway, a road which ends at Rocky Point Bay, a popular boat launch area on the lake. Davy told him there was a storm coming in and specifically told him to stay at the parking area until the storm had passed. He asked Jake about the boat they were using. Jake calmed his father by stating, "We have a lot better boat now, Dad!". Davy wanted to make sure they were using a good quality boat if they were going out on the lake. Jake assured Davy they would stay on land until the storm had moved through the area.

It was Saturday morning and I had plans of painting their bathroom, putting up a new mirror and hanging a new towel rack. I got up early and staged all my equipment and materials for the day's project. I prepped all the trim with a caulk gun. I had the paint stirred and ready to begin painting. And then suddenly it was as if a dark heavy weight came upon me. I could not shake it. The feeling was so heavy and oppressive I closed the paint can. I left the bathroom and walked into the den. I had a deep troubling spirit within me. I instinctively began to call Jake's cell phone. There was no answer. I tried again and still no answer. I sat in the den recliner crippled with fear. Something was wrong, and I could feel it in my heart.

Davy was working the 12-hour night shift and he woke up early and walked into the den. He said, "I thought you were painting the bathroom today?" I explained I was prepping the bathroom to paint it and then I got a horrible feeling something bad was wrong. I explained to him I was trying to reach Jake's cell phone, but he was not answering. He remarked to me, "Jake is out on the water and his phone is in the truck at the dock parking area. He will call once he gets back to his truck." He continued to tell me everything was okay. "Lori, you are worrying yourself for nothing. Everything is okay. It is still early, and those boys are duck hunting."

I continued to leave messages on Jake's cell phone begging him to call me and let me know he was okay. I continued to tell Davy things did not feel right and something was bad wrong. He said, "Jake will call you when they are off the lake and finished duck hunting. You have to stop worrying!"

He insisted everything was fine and I was just driving myself crazy. I continued with nagging anxiety. To get my mind off the situation he said, "Go get dressed and let's go out to eat in Paducah. We will drive separately, and I will leave for work afterward and you and Hunter can come back home." I reluctantly showered and got dressed. As time passed my worries increased. I got dressed and got Hunter ready. They rode together in his car and I followed along behind them. I was glad I was alone in the car because I could continue trying to contact Jake. I still couldn't reach him. We made our way down the long and winding roads as we traveled towards Paducah. We made our way onto the West I-24 ramp leading to the interstate. As I topped the hill just past the Husband's Road exit, I saw the convoy of emergency vehicles with their lights on traveling toward us, moving east on I-24. It was the Paducah-McCracken County Rescue Squad and they were hauling a search and rescue boat. Upon the mere recognition of the boat, I felt as if I had been punched in the stomach. I called Davy on his cell phone and told him, "Davy, listen to me! I am telling you something is wrong! You saw that convoy go past us. I know it and I cannot explain it to you, but Jake is in trouble and I can feel it! That was the rescue squad with a boat. Davy, I am telling you something is wrong!" He continued to deny it and continued to tell me Jake was fine.

I tried to calm myself before calling my mother. I knew she would be near a desktop computer. I did not tell her my suspicions, but I told her I needed her to go to her desktop computer and look up the local *WPSD* news on their website and see if there was any breaking news. As I waited in silence while she made her way to her computer and the website, I took deep breaths, but my heart was racing. My mother said, "ok, I see here on *WPSD* there is breaking news of duck hunters missing on Kentucky Lake." I felt as if my heart was pounding into my throat. I quickly hung up the phone. I then called Jake's best friend, Taylor, and asked if he had heard from Jake. He said he had not spoken to him. I told him about the news story. I told him I was sick with worry and if he spoke to Jake to please tell him to call me immediately. We arrived at the restaurant. I called my mother-in-law and asked her for the phone number to the local Marshall County Hospital. I contacted the local hospital and left my number for them to call me back if they heard anything about Jake. My phone rang, and it was Taylor. Taylor said, "Mrs. Lori, it is Jake they are looking for." I don't even remember what I said to Taylor, but I hung up immediately. All my instincts had become a reality. We rushed out of the restaurant and I could hardly walk my knees were so weak. Once in the parking area, I began to scream. Davy had to physically place me in the passenger's side of the car after picking me up out of the parking lot. Davy left his work car in the parking lot. While driving at a high rate of speed and with caution lights flashing on I-24 east, my cell phone rang. It was the Marshall County Emergency Management team and she told me we needed to report to the East Marshall Fire Department. I knew where the fire department was located because it was only a few miles from my in-law's home off Moors Campground Road. She continued to say they were searching for the boys. She asked me to take a deep breath and to drive slowly. She explained to me that one boy, Tyler, tried to swim to safety and a neighbor heard him calling for help. He was rescued by the neighbor with his boat. He was in the hospital recovering from severe hypothermia. She said they would update us further on the search when we reached the fire department. My world was collapsing around me. My motherly instinct was right!

We learned the winds picked up unexpectedly as the boys were crossing Kentucky Lake (more than 1.5 miles across) to make their way back to Rocky Point Bay. The abrupt change of wind direction came suddenly upon the lake, rushing fiercely across the lake's surface. The waves grew taller and taller. With 2-3 foot white-capping waves, water filled the boat. The boys pulled the boat's plug and gunned the boat to attempt to remove the water and make it to the bay. As the winds raged, the waves grew. The boat struck another set of waves, engulfing it. The boat capsized. All four boys were in the cold sharp winter water of Kentucky Lake. It was too far across the lake and the water was frigid. With water temperatures in the 40's, Tyler set out to swim to safety to get help for everyone. Within a few minutes, hypothermia became the enemy of life for the three boys. The weather which brought the wind and the waves became my foe. I cursed the elements with all my might!

The Search

We arrived at the East Marshall Fire Department. Soon after we arrived word began to spread. Friends, family, and acquaintances began to fill the building. Volunteers of the fire department came and offered their assistance. Church vans arrived one by one unloading food and supplies. The first church van to arrive was from the church I attended as a youth, the same church where Davy and I were married, and the church where my sister attended. The van was packed with food and supplies. My Sunday school teacher from my youth, Mrs. Pat, came and served the families and the search and rescue workers. Not only did this van bring food and supplies, but it also carried the fruit of compassion as it ministered to the families and volunteers.

More volunteers began arriving and coordinating searches on foot around the lake's perimeter. Additional volunteers arrived with their personal boats to search the water for any sign of the boys. Men and women on horseback took part in the search.

Mckenzie's boat, a pair of waders, some life vests, and miscellaneous hunting supplies had been discovered. The coroner and emergency management entered the fire department following the conclusion of the first day's search and provided an update to the families.

The day was a horror-filled nightmare. The bad news continued. We wanted nothing more than to wake up and it all be a bad dream. We went home but there was no way we could sleep knowing our Jake was gone and there was no sign of him or his friends, Trevor and Mckenzie.

On day 2 we went back to the search site at Rocky Point Bay of Kentucky Lake. The crews held a morning briefing. Each morning the search began with a group prayer. The *Red Cross* disaster team arrived and served the rescue workers and families. An outpouring of volunteers donated hand warmers, foot warmers, gloves, hot chocolate, food, propane heaters, blankets, coveralls, fuel, and other daily needs. Soon the bay parking area was filled with dive teams, boats, volunteers, rescue teams, and emergency management personnel. Saw-horse barricades were set up to keep on-lookers out of the area and allow additional search teams to park. People offering encouragement stood in line to get to the areas where the families were located within the pavilion. The media made repeated calls and appearances asking for interviews. We had been painfully thrust into the midst of the largest historical search and rescue in Western Kentucky.

Thirty hours into the search, on Sunday evening, Trevor's body was recovered. His family could now plan on a funeral and burial for him. According to professional rescue and recovery teams, we were informed Jake and Mckenzie would be close to where Trevor was located. It was late and the day's search was called off for the evening.

In future days, there was a large covered picnic area (pavilion) which was tarped off with plastic to keep the harsh January winds out. What was once a fun picnic area for families had become a makeshift warming area for the families and recovery workers. Propane heaters were positioned inside. Volunteers and local churches filled the pavilion with food and supplies each day. Volunteers helped serve food throughout the day, serving breakfast, lunch, and dinner. Davy and I positioned ourselves on the bay watching the boats on the water, then visiting the pavilion to warm our hands and feet as needed. We just kept hoping for any sign of activity continually anxious for news.

The harsh January winds and frigid temperatures continued. The weather became our enemy. I cursed the weather forecast almost daily. I depended upon the forecast. The wind speeds became my new fixation. The search and rescue revolved around the forecast. I couldn't control it. It was outside my power! I was helpless!

To shorten our daily drive, we took up a temporary residence with my in-laws at their lake house. Late at night, the lights glistened off the water allowing me to watch the water from the patio windows. Watching the height of the waves became my obsession wondering if a search could resume the following day. I hoped for calm waters allowing boats to be on the water.

The news media outlets were reporting the boy's boat capsized due to 2-3 foot whitecaps. Social media became a zoo where rumors, speculations, and "Monday morning quarterbacks" took front stage. There was no one who wanted to go back and change the course of events more than Davy and myself. If we could rewind, we certainly would not have allowed

19

Jake to go duck hunting on the lake. If only we were perfect people who always made perfect decisions. If we could have reverted, we would have kept him at home that fateful day. If only we could go back…if only we could go back! We found ourselves repetitively rewinding our decisions and the pain was consuming our energy. If only life afforded us the opportunity to go back in time and change our decisions!

Day 3 came and left us once again empty-handed. As the workweek continued volunteers had to return to normal jobs so search activity was scaled back. Faithfully, many individuals used vacation time or applied for special leave to help. Day 4 came. Still no sign of the boys. The frigid temperatures and winds continued halting searches on many occasions. It was too dangerous for the search crews. Rescue workers were put in danger of their boats capsizing as they took on water during times of gusting winds.

When searches could resume, an ambulance was set up as a warming center for divers suffering from hypothermic symptoms. We watched as divers returned to surface and crawled inside the boat only to freeze to the side of the boat. Those returning to the shore banks had ice frozen in their beards or mustaches. Daily, the workers sacrificed themselves to the harsh winter conditions.

Yes, the weather was our rival. All I could think about is how the wind cost Jake and his friends their lives, and now the winds and freezing temperatures were delaying and hurting the search mission. I detested the weather! Each night we checked the forecast for tomorrow's windspeeds with our hopes being either let down or grasping at a chance for the search to resume.

Trevor's funeral visitation was held at his high school gymnasium. Davy and I left the lake and made our trip back to Mayfield to the visitation. I recall us having conversations about the boys and memories of them. We scanned the car radio from station to station as we waited for the top of the hour news. As we pulled into the parking lot at Trevor's visitation the parking lot was full of cars. The song, *"Feed Jake"*[4] started to play on the radio. We both sat in the car before the visitation and wept uncontrollably and could not help but smile through the tears. We both accredited the song to Jake comforting his parents. We had to remain in the parking lot sitting in the car as we dried our eyes and tried to recover from this emotional outpouring. We both knew this was no coincidence. We had not heard the song in years.

Additional teams arrived with search dogs to walk the banks of the lake. A yellow Labrador search and rescue dog named Rosco specially trained to conduct water searches arrived from Tennessee with his owner and trainer, Robin. He had served in recovery efforts following Hurricane Katrina in 2005. Not only did Rosco arrive to ride in the boats during the search, but after they were finished on the water, our son, Hunter, who was six years old at the time would pet Rosco. This took Hunter's mind off all the surrounding sadness. He fell in love with this dog. Rosco was good therapy for Hunter and for our family. Additional search dogs arrived from Tennessee and Kentucky.

Word spread into the tri-state area of Kentucky, Illinois, and Missouri. Phone calls came in from local representatives and lawmakers. Word spread to Texas offering professional dive teams. Requests were made to our governor for additional assistance and special equipment.

I recall a day I was waiting by the bay amid a crowd of volunteers in the parking area. A lady (a stranger to me) had been standing in line waiting to see me. She had to park a distance from the volunteer area barricaded by sawhorses. She had a piece of paper folded up and she quickly handed it to me. She placed it in my hands and then placed both of her hands over my hands pressing them together tightly in a loving fashion. She veered straight into my eyes, then closed her eyes in a moment of pause. Inside the piece of paper was a handwritten message: *"...for truly I say to you, if you have faith the size of a mustard seed, you will say to this mountain, 'Move from here to there,' and it will move; and nothing will be impossible to you."* (Matthew 17:20 NAS) A mustard seed was taped inside the folded paper under the Bible verse. The lady felt it very important for me to have this note and to meditate upon the verse and its meaning. I thanked her and she made her way back to her vehicle.

We had a huge support group, but we also had doubters who told us the boys would not be discovered until water temperatures rose. Others wanted to remind us the boys may have already been swept through the Kentucky Dam which was visible upstream from Rocky Point Bay (3.9 nautical miles).

Those with sonar equipment informed us of the rough bottom terrain of Kentucky Lake. This meant it was sometimes difficult to obtain clear sonar images. The lake was a man-made lake created in the early 1940s by the Tennessee Valley Authority. It is the largest artificial lake by surface area in the United States east of the Mississippi River. When TVA flooded the area any structure which stood in the way was submerged under Kentucky Lake.[5] This is different from a smooth slate-bottom River.

Funds were donated by the community to provide a helicopter search of the Kentucky Lake. Dye packs were placed in the water to study the ebb and flow of the lake. A large dragging operation was set up focusing on the coordinates where Trevor's body was recovered.

A special crew of "hard hat divers" joined in the search. They were unlike scuba divers. The hard hat divers wear special weighted boots allowing them to walk the bottom of the lake and maneuver the rough topography beneath the surface of the water. We came to know Herb, the hard hat diver from Tennessee. Herb returned on his days off from his normal job, scanning the water depths with the sonar equipment. He had a larger boat equipped with an overhead cab. He maneuvered the boat back and forth over search grids watching for any image popping up on his radar worthy of suiting up for a dive. Herb mapped coordinates and planned his search grid. His trained eye knew how to spot a body on a side-scan sonar screen. He had learned the hard way—through the recovery of other bodies throughout his career. I continued to place my hope in the scanning equipment. I held onto hope for the day of their discovery. The reality was Jake was not coming home to us alive, but there was no way we would allow him to be undiscovered. We vowed to stay at this lake until both Jake and Mckenzie were found.

Word spread to an outside agency, the Seth Foundation. I spoke regularly to the founder, Sheila, who began the foundation after she lost her son in a water sporting accident. Her family encountered problems trying to locate his body. From her personal and tragic learnings, she came to guide other families going through the same struggles and barriers. She offered guidance and most of all support through sharing her experiences. This mother's pain became her passion and her purpose. She engaged divers and sonar equipment operators to form a supportive network offering aid where needed.

My days were consumed with watching the boats go out and the boats return without our boys. I asked God to please let today be the day He would bring the boys home to us. Sometimes I sat on the rocks by the water and stared out in a daze. One day while sitting quietly on the bay watching the crews at work, four Canadian Geese flew over me. They were loud and flew low over the bank of the Kentucky Lake as they honked and caught my attention. I couldn't help but watch these majestic creatures. The three flew ahead and one goose drifted back in behind them. I couldn't help but think about the three boys who left the earth, and Tyler, the sole survivor and the trauma he was going through witnessing such a horrible event. He was sure to be forever changed. Life as he once knew it was in the past. All the families involved in the horrific January 10th day were forever altered. There was no return to the life we once called familiar.

The geese returned to Rocky Point on many occasions and I always felt a comforting feeling as I watched them closely fly overhead and then disappear into the distance. I did not pay attention to the geese prior to losing Jake.

One evening Trevor's dad, Clay, coordinated a search on Kentucky Lake. Clay had a boat and proclaimed, "the last thing I can do for my son is to find his two best friends." He was relentless and focused.

On some evenings the nighttime was the best time to search the lake because of decreased wind speeds. His friends and families had their own personal boats and we used basic sonar "fish finders" to scan for images. We watched the coordinates of the lake and scanned for images. If we saw something suspicious, we re-scanned the water until we had either eliminated it as a possibility or marked it for further review. I rode in the boat with a friend of the family and watched the sonar camera closely looking for any image which appeared human-like. We returned to the dock as the fog was getting heavy. We could barely see glimmers of light. They quickly faded as the fog consumed the illuminations. Davy and Trevor's uncle continued to scan the water as the fog grew denser. They got lost and went in circles. The fog was overcoming. They trolled back and forth only to end up once again in front of the large radio tower on the bank directly across from Rocky Point dock area. They re-launched hoping to get back to the dock and somehow ended up again in front of the large radio tower. Davy remarked, "We are going in a circle! How are we just circling back to the same point?" They gained a point of reference with the radio tower knowing Rocky Point was across the bay and then decided to steer straight across the lake until they were back to the other side. I was back on the bank, so I turned on the truck headlights, so they could use the rays to make their way back. Our friends used a spotlight and truck lights to send a beacon out for them. Finally, they were able to reach the correct bay. I certainly now understood the importance of a lighthouse for sailors in the days before the invention of high-tech navigation equipment.

At the end of January, we were informed *The Weather Channel* meteorologist, *Jim Cantore*, was coming to Paducah due to an anticipated crippling ice storm for the region. Paducah was 30 minutes from our home. We watched as the search and rescue teams loaded up and began to leave one by one. What was once the largest search and rescue mission in Western Kentucky was now an empty parking lot. Yes, Western Kentucky was now expecting an epic ice storm. Volunteers left to prepare their homes, to purchase fuel, set up generators, and to stock up on emergency supplies as the weather forecasters cautioned of potential massive long-term power outages.

Upon learning about the oncoming ice storm, I remember the boiling rage mounting inside me. As soon as I was alone the rage erupted. I broke! I cried out to God. I remember in my disgruntled brokenness telling God, "bad just wasn't bad enough, now You have to send an ice storm?" I was angry with God and had been since that fateful January 10th morning. I told Him I knew it was me He wanted but questioned why He took Jake away. "Jake was young, and You should have taken me! Why Jake? I cried." I was consumed with fury! I was exhausted with desperation!

At the beginning of the search, we met the fire department chaplain, Pastor Mike. He came to the search often to check-in with each family and offer comfort and encouragement. He was a kind and gentle man. He held frequent prayers with the group, praying for safety and protection of the recovery workers, the comfort for the families, and for the boys to be found soon.

The eve of the approaching ice storm I left and made my way to our home in Hickory. Davy stayed behind at Rocky Point packing up equipment and protecting things from the elements. The evening was a rare opportunity for Pastor Mike and Davy to speak in private. The crowds left. Pastor Mike shared with Davy the divorce statistics of couples who lose children. He explained grief was tough on a marriage, explaining everyone grieves differently-- sometimes the man grieves in one way and the woman grieves in a different way. The divorce statistics vary but undeniably the statistics are high for couples who lose a child. He explained to Davy to keep the family together. At one point in the conversation, Davy said he looked at him and said, "What kind of man are you going to be?" Davy remembers and recalls their private conversation and his lesson to him about the family unit grieving together in unity. As Davy recalls, the two of them being able to speak privately during the search was a memorable moment.

Just as forecasters predicted the ice storm came causing wide-spread damage to Western Kentucky. Early the next morning it sounded like guns going off in the surrounding woods as ice limbs became weighted down from the thick ice. Limbs broke, trees fell, power and telephone lines sagged. Trees fell on homes. Extensive devastating power outages crippled the area. Many roads were impassable because of downed trees and power lines. This was the largest ice storm in the history of the region. Through the devastation, our minds were fixed on Jake and Mckenzie being found. However, we were forced to pause and set up a generator to hook up to the refrigerator and freezer to preserve our food. We had two gas log fireplaces enabling us to section off rooms of the home to keep warm. Heartily, our focus was getting back to the lake as quickly as possible. This storm was a huge inconvenience. It was delaying crews being able to return to the water. The emergency management teams had no choice but to focus on getting their counties restored and operating once again.

The infamous ice storm of 2009 paid no favors to anyone. With power outages families needed bottled water, food, fuel for generators, propane bottles or cylinders for setting up cooking stations. There was no word on how long it would take for power to be restored. The governor responded quickly declaring a state of emergency allowing the National Guard to deliver water and supplies. We cooked on a propane camp stove. Neighbors helped neighbors by sharing food and supplies. There is nothing like a crisis to bring out the best in people and the community. One day following the ice storm, Trevor's dad made his way back to the lake with his boat to begin scanning the water with donated sonar equipment.

Once again, the weather was our enemy and I blamed the Creator of the weather, God, for this wide-spread devastation. Hopeless and helpless, the anger did not change our circumstances.

Our pastor, Bro. Ronnie, made many trips to visit with us during the search and recovery operation. He not only checked on our spiritual needs but our physical needs. The church congregation through the goodness of their hearts donated money to purchase search and recovery equipment. Other individuals and agencies joined in the efforts. Benefit concerts and community fund-raisers were held to aid in supporting search efforts for food, gas, heating, lodging, equipment, special personal protective equipment, etc. The aid was overwhelming confirming there are many good and kind-hearted people in this world. There was a generous flood of volunteers desiring to serve in needed capacities.

During his visits, Bro. Ronnie commonly stated, "Is there anything you all need? Can you think of anything we can get or have done? We might not have it, but we might be able to find someone who does. We just want to be a help and be a source of encouragement to you all as you go through these dark days. The church really wants to help."

Those statements were shattering ideas I had formed about the church from my youth. They were redefining the church for me. The church was resembling a hand reaching out to help us. It was becoming a lifeline to me, offering to carry the weight of some of my problems. The building of brick and mortar was coming to life. Yes, the church was becoming more than just a building structure to me. It was becoming more than just rules and laws. We had been plunged into a dire position of overwhelming need. No amount of money could solve our heartbreak. We were swimming in an ocean of bad news and hopelessness.

During one trip, Bro. Ronnie made a weighty statement. His short decree stuck with me. It grabbed me, and it jolted me. (Chances are good he probably did not realize it impacted me so deeply.) He made this statement: "On days when you are down, go and help someone". Whoa! Resentment almost welled up within me. I thought to myself, "How can I go and help anyone? In my grief-stricken state, I can barely help myself or care for the needs of Hunter." I was finding it difficult to even brush my teeth or perform routine tasks to get ready each morning. My mind was running in different directions. Focusing was exhausting. And so, with all this pondering, the statement weighed heavily and stirred within me. I was having trouble seeing a future where I would be able to help anyone in their time of anguish.

We had high hopes for a team assigned to the search from northern Kentucky. However, due to equipment problems and illness, time on the water was limited. Davy and I were at an all-time low. One disappointment was followed by another bigger disappointment. Those voices doubting the boys would be recovered increased. The voices encouraging us to let go were growing in number. Everything seemed to be stacked against us. I became restless and continued daily without good sleep. I went to bed crying and awoke crying. Many days I felt numb. Some mistakenly analyzed my numbness as strength. I was weak in every way. The numbness only came from being in a trance-like state from the continued crushing blows to us since the deadly day. I could not deal with any more negative news!

I went home the evening of February 23rd, 44 days into the search. By this point I was suffering from extreme exhaustion. I was at the end of my rope! It seemed as if everything was imploding around me. We were in a helpless and hopeless situation. No amount of money could bring the boys home. No amount of effort could bring success to the search. The overwhelming desperateness brought me to my knees. There was no one I could turn to, but God. I began to cry out to God in the privacy of my bedroom. I told God I knew He had been chasing me most of my life. I could feel His pull upon my heart. I had been too afraid to get close to Him. It seemed as if every time I had tried to get close to Him, something bad happened to me. And so, I had blamed Him for all of life's struggles since childhood. I told Him, "I give in! I am all yours now!" I surrendered to Him every part of my life and I promised and vowed to serve Him all the days of my life. I told Him I was giving Him full control over every part of my life. I cried out to Him to please be willing to let us bring our boys home to bury. But, sobbing tearfully, I told Him if He chose not to allow us to find Jake it was something I would not like, but I would have to learn to accept. I turned all the search and rescue efforts over to Him. I explained to Him I would serve Him regardless of the recovery outcome. I repented asking Him to forgive me of my very sinful rebellious past. I had run from Him out of fear for 39 years. I had been raised in the church but knowingly lived a lifestyle unpleasing to God's commandments. I was the lord of my life and on February 23rd I made Jesus the Lord of my heart.

I do not remember falling asleep. I slept all night without waking once. It was the best sleep I had in ages. There was something different in my state of mind. Words couldn't explain how different I felt. The feelings of nervousness, anxiousness, and hopelessness were all gone. There are no words to define the newly discovered peace. I made peace with God for the first time in my life. My son was in the cold waters of Kentucky Lake, yet I had an unexplainable calmness. How could this be? It did not make sense to me. I wanted to tell Davy but was hesitant. How could I make him comprehend when I didn't understand? How could I even begin the conversation with what I had just experienced?

Various telephone messages had been left with the Kentucky governor's office requesting additional help with recovery prior to the ice storm. We were shocked to learn more help was in progress. The Department of Homeland Security was given oversight of the search coordinating efforts with the Illinois Department of Natural Resources. The Illinois team equipped with a high-tech side-scan sonar arrived and began their search. This was the same team present the day Trevor was discovered. Another volunteer team, *Team Watters*, came with their boat and sonar equipment. "Hard hat diver", Herb, from Tennessee and an area diver, Gary, traveled to Rocky Point to join the day's search.

We prepared to make our long trip back to the site on the morning of February 24, 2009. We had only traveled a few miles down the road. I could not contain my feelings any longer to Davy. I explained to him today I had a whole new peaceful feeling. I told him, "Wouldn't it be great, Davy, if the peace and comfort I am feeling today mean today is our day?" Davy responded to me as I told him about my whole-hearted peaceful feeling, "I hope you are right." (I felt like maybe he was listening to me a little more about my instincts since January 10th). I shared with him a song I had picked out for the funeral during our trip back to the lake. I was making plans as if we would find the boys. We both cried, and a small but warm smile erupted through the tears on our faces. We held hands in the truck as we made the journey back to Rocky Point. I felt a special renewed kind of closeness to him and I will never forget the long drive back to the bay.

We arrived at Rocky Point. This was now day 45 of the search. We met with the Illinois Department of Natural Resource crews and discussed the search grid and their plans for the day. The water was calm. The day went much like many other days where we watched the boats maneuver back and forth across the lake slowly. It was very strange and hard to explain: never in all my life could I explain or understand the peace at one of the most tragic times of my life. I felt rested and I felt strengthened at the same time. This was not something others could comprehend. It was a mystery even to me.

We watched the boats work then go to break, and then to lunch. They worked diligently and did not offer any updates during the day. At approximately 4:00 p.m. a state employee came and knocked on our truck window as we sat in the bay parking lot. He explained things to us. He told us he knew this was a tough search. He wanted to "manage our expectations". He clarified there were two points of interest the teams felt were worthy of diving for further review. He desired us to know we would see activity occurring and to be aware of what was happening. He wanted us to understand the images may be nothing. He restated once again he strived to "manage our expectations" and not "give false hope". We thanked him for communicating to us. We both sat anxiously as we saw *Team Watters'* boat return to the dock for anchors and rope. We waited patiently as the team gathered their supplies and rushed back out to the other boats located just in front of the radio tower opposite Rocky Point. Soon, Officer Frank returned to our truck and said, "We have one boy!" I turned to Davy and said "I know that's Mckenzie. It's not Jake. I just know it!" A few minutes later Officer Frank returned to our truck and said, "We have two boys!"

I got out of the truck, slid down the side of the vehicle, and fell to my knees on the asphalt pavement thanking God. There was a surge of emotions springing forth. We cried and sobbed bittersweet tears. Family and friends began arriving. People began calling us as word spread of the discovery of the boys. From a distance across the bay, I watched as the Kentucky Game and Wildlife boat went to retrieve our boys. As you gaze across Rocky Point Bay to the other side of the lake, there stood the radio tower. That massive steel structure had been our point of reference and our lighthouse during those foggy evenings of search.

I stood on the dock and waited patiently to meet the diver who brought the boys to surface. As the boats pulled to the dock, the team came and offered hugs. We thanked them for their hard work and dedication. The diver who recovered the boys, still dressed in his attire, with tears in his eyes looked at me. I could see the happiness in his expression but the sadness too. I thanked him. He seemed frozen and only glassy-eyed. I will never forget the look in those eyes. In front of me stood the man who had held my son's lifeless body. I paused in the bittersweet moment and

33

gazed out across the still quiet waters of glass on Kentucky Lake. For the first time in weeks, we knew where Jake was located!

On this 45th day, I was beginning to learn God's true nature rather than the one I misdefined throughout my life. I thought to myself about the goodness of God. He knew when I was serious about my commitment to Him. He knew! I believe God had shown His grace to me. On February 23rd, I had made peace with God through His Son, Jesus Christ, and now God was showing me His true nature on February 24th. I surrendered my heart at Rocky Point! A deep spiritual awakening was occurring inside me: God is the last to be praised but He is the first to be blamed. I was convicted by my own past shallowness. So many times, I believed I was waiting on God, but God was waiting on me for a real and full surrender to Him. I believed He was showing His love toward me. All my life I was taught that God loved me. But, on this day I felt a very warm love and I felt God was near and present.

Herb and his team later attended the funeral visitation for Jake on February 27, 2009. We laid Jake to rest on February 28th on the quiet hillside of our church's cemetery. Then, we attended Mckenzie's visitation, funeral, and burial. Herb explained to us he was working in between two different searches, Mr. Moffett, from Savannah, TN, and our boys. Now that our search was completed, he could resume assisting in the Savannah recovery.

Caregiver

In the days following Jake's burial, I went to the mailbox and discovered a large yellow business envelope addressed to my attention from his company. What I found inside stunned me to the core. It was a letter addressed to me from his employer stating what a wonderful boy and employee Jacob had been while working for them. Then she proceeded to inform me in the letter he had taken out a life insurance policy on himself. She explained the level of maturity he possessed to see this as a necessity. I read this again and again as I tried to understand and grasp all of this. He worked a part-time job after school, and he had taken out a life insurance policy on himself. How could this be? Jake was the type to work hard and yet was very intent on saving every penny. He was 17 years old and a senior in high school and he had taken out life insurance? This was only a part-time job and we were not aware he had benefits.

After reading the letter from his employer I laid across the steering wheel in the car weeping. This child took care of his family even in his death. The depth of Jake's maturity, the level of compassion and concern for others was above and beyond any ordinary 17-year old boy.

As the days passed, we learned other stories about our Jake. One fellow student reported to us: he carried the books of a disabled girl to her classroom for her. This act describes the warmth and care of our Jake and further illustrates the young boy we knew and loved so much.

Jacob's friends told us, "When you had Jacob as a friend, you had a real friendship!". There was a special kind of love in that 17-year old warm heart. Oh, how I miss him! He was so warm and gentle. His absence.... a permanent painful reality!

We learned of the search for Mr. Moffett of Savannah, Tennessee from Herb. The old Savannah, Tennessee bridge was demolished following the opening of the new bridge. Some of the old bridge features were still beneath the water. I searched online for a news article regarding the search. I took a keen interest in researching to see if his body had been recovered. Herb told us the Savannah search was much different than Rocky Point because of the underwater terrain. The Tennessee River at Savannah was a smooth slate bottom river and because of the narrowness of the river at the bridge's location, the water current was dangerously swift.

Courier Newspaper, Savannah, Tennessee reported on February 9, 2009:

Monday morning, the body of a man who leaped to his apparent death from the Tennessee River bridge at Savannah on Friday had yet to be recovered. Hardin County Fire Chief Melvin Martin identified the victim as Timothy Eugene Moffett, 47, of Airport Road in McNairy County. He is the second Moffett to die in the river in less than a year. His son, Timothy Dexter Moffett, was 18 when he drowned about 50 feet from shore while swimming in the Tennessee near River Heights Restaurant in Crump on May 4. Martin said the elder Moffett jumped from the bridge's eastbound lanes around 7:30 a.m. A bus driver for the Hardin County school system was a witness, he said. Hardin County Director of Schools John Thomas said the driver told him she "saw a man just step up on the edge there. There wasn't any standing and thinking about it. It was just one, two, three." A large-scale dragging effort was initiated to recover Moffett's body.

Martin said it included in addition to the Hardin County Rescue Squad, members of volunteer squads from Decatur, Hardeman, Perry, Humphries, Obion, Fayette, Henry and Chester counties, and the city of Humboldt in Gibson County. Rescue workers were on the water minutes after Moffett's leap and dragging operations were mounted throughout the weekend, he said.

But for now, recovery operations have been scaled back. "We're not quitting," said Martin. "We'll have somebody out there every day. If we don't find anything by Friday, we plan to resume dragging operations."[6]

Following Jake's funeral, I took some additional time off to rest before returning to work. My boss was fully supportive of me easing myself back into the office. A few weeks after returning to work, I received a call from Sheila at the Seth Foundation. She asked if I was ready and strong enough to help someone. She explained how there was incredible healing in helping others. She was coordinating the necessary resources to go to the Savannah recovery operation. I told her I would speak to Trevor's father, Clay, and see if we could make a trip to Savannah on Saturday and scan the river. She was planning to have divers in the area the following weekend. She explained since they knew the point of Mr. Moffett's entry to the water, the search would be straight-forward.

I contacted Clay and he was quick to respond "Yes, we will load up early and make the trip!". All three families of the boys made the two-and-a-half-hour trip to Savannah on Saturday, March 21st. As soon as we reached the Savannah bridge I looked to my right and there sat a woman all alone in a fold-out chair beside the banks of the Tennessee River. I will never forget the lonely and despairing look of her just sitting there waiting—waiting for anyone, waiting for help, waiting for a sign, and clinging to hope. I could certainly empathize with her. We parked the truck and introduced ourselves. Clay and Davy launched the boat and began to scan beneath the bridge. While they were scanning, I was able to speak further with her about our search and recovery struggles on Kentucky Lake. My heart ached for her. She lost her teenage son and now her husband. Those two tragedies were too much for the mind to comprehend. Of course, we knew all too well, without a body to bury there is no closure. There is only searching and hoping. Oh, could I understand and put myself right back on Rocky Point Bay again! She had lost her soulmate as well as her son and this was more than I could ponder within my mind—so much loss for her and in such a quick time frame! My mind could not process such a great loss.

In only a few minutes, Clay and Davy returned to the boat launch. Clay said "This is not at all what we were dealing with on Kentucky Lake. This river is a slate-bottom river and the current is swifter than I anticipated." He explained they were getting some additional supplies and then returning to the water. He explained they would travel further up the river and begin looking for places where the body might be entangled in debris. While they were still on the bank, my cell phone rang. It was Sheila from the foundation. She asked if I was with Mrs. Moffett. Sheila informed me a couple of crappie fishermen about three miles from where we were located found the body. She asked me to wait with Mrs. Moffett. The fire chief would be the one to officially notify the family. I sat quietly waiting. I informed Davy and Clay they did not have to return to the water as his body was being recovered upriver. Mrs. Moffett's daughter needed their vehicle, so she took her mother to the search site and then left to run her errands. Therefore, Mrs. Moffett had no transportation to the morgue. As soon as the fire chief notified her, we transported her to the morgue located within the county hospital to meet with officials. We sat with her as friends and family gathered offering hugs. Her pastor soon arrived to be with the family. I was reminded of the evening of the boy's bittersweet homecoming. My heart felt heavy as an official entered the room carrying the wedding band of her husband. It took me back to the day I finally retrieved the items which were in Jake's pockets the day he died. I still have those things wrapped in a Ziploc bag in a keepsake box. It is a box I don't intend to open. There is a mountain of pain inside that white box. That box has remained closed.

We loaded up and made the long trip back to Mayfield. I recalled what Bro. Ronnie told us before our boys had been discovered, "When you are down, go help someone." And, now this meant so much more to me! I saw the events of the day as no coincidence: Three families brought together at Rocky Point were in a town two- and one-half hours away on the exact day Mr. Moffett's body was recovered. I was learning there is no such thing as coincidence! We went to help someone, and God rewarded us with a blessing money could not purchase. His body was recovered and now his wife could begin the process of healing. Tears of joy streamed down my face! We knew the emotional release which occurs when their body is located after a lengthy search mission.

During the trip back home, I contacted Bro. Ronnie and shared the news with him. The next day at church at the end of his sermon he told the story and asked me to come to the front and share the story with the congregation. I was too overwhelmed with emotion to share the story. I couldn't keep from crying. My voice was quivering too much for the congregation to understand what I was saying. And so, I sat in my seat as he told the story sobbing uncontrollably. I am not sure Bro. Ronnie knew what a realization I was experiencing on that spring day in 2009. The profound statement he made at Rocky Point caused rebellion to rise within my core. However, this same declaration became a great source of comfort, healing, and blessing. If I had rejected his instruction, I would have missed the overwhelming blessing of Mr. Moffett's discovery.

I believed God was reinforcing to me the blessings of helping others and sharing His love with the hurting. I could look back and see how He was using us to comfort others. I began to see a glimpse of purpose in my own life. When our eyes are continually focused on our own pain, we not only hinder our own healing process, but we miss out on blessings. It was an epic moment. As I look back over the years, I see Savannah, Tennessee as a spiritual marker in my journey. It was challenging me to dig deeper inside to see what else God had in store for me as I surrendered my personal agenda to His will.

"I have heard of You by the hearing of the ear, But now my eye sees You."

Job 42:5 (NKJV)

From my Rocky Point experiences, I have learned principles which have proven themselves time and time again.

Rocky Point Principles:

"When you are hurting, go out and help someone.

There is a blessing in it somewhere."—Bro. Ronnie Stinson, Sr.

When you believe in Jesus Christ

your eyes are open to the spiritual.

Rebellion delays the heart's healing.

A heart open to God is open to healing.

The Church is the body of Christ reaching out to the lost and the broken

strengthening them together with the same love Christ poured into them.

The true Church is on the move.

Monumental Moment

In May 2009, community contributors donated funds for a monument to be placed on the banks of Rocky Point. The monument honored the volunteers of the search mission as well as Jacob, Mckenzie, and Trevor.

Friends and families gathered on the bank for a time of remembrance and prayer. Pastor Mike returned to the scene leading the group in prayer. As those who were gathered bowed their heads in prayer, three Canadian Geese came flying low honking right in the middle of the prayer. Everyone stopped, opened their eyes and watched them fly over. Even Pastor Mike looked back over his right shoulder as we watched them fly away and their sound travel into the distance. Once again, these three geese brought some serene comfort. I bowed my head as we continued to pray, and I felt the spring breeze sweep across my face. My heart was warmed from the appearance of the geese. I was relating my Creator's control of all His many creations. His timing was indeed perfect. He was near!

"For where two or three are gathered together in My name, there am I in the midst of them." Matthew 18:20 KJV

"The Lord is near to the brokenhearted and saves those who are crushed in spirit." Psalm 34:18 NAS

Rocky Point Principle:

God brings comfort to the grieving in a

specific and unique way.

God is in control of all His creations.

A Comforting Twist

After losing Jake and enduring the agonizing 45-day search and recovery, I finally found the strength to return to my job as plant manager of a dairy processing plant. Looking back, I believed if I kept my mind busy on my job, I could overcome the grief. I was using the demands of the job as my therapy. This led to a recurring pattern of exhaustion. I was not dealing with grief in a healthy manner.

There were many days my yearning for Jake was so severe it felt as if I had a 50-pound weight on my shoulders. The cloud of darkness caused intense doubting. Many nights, I cried myself to sleep only to awake crying. I doubted I could ever be content again. I doubted today. I doubted tomorrow. I doubted a future. I doubted hope.

It was hard to think about anything. My mind raced, and my heart missed Jake. I really did not think I would be able to make it through yet another day of work. It was a battle each day just to get myself ready for work and my son ready for school. Yet, when I arrived at work it was almost therapeutic. The day's demands always managed to keep me busy answering questions, traveling from one meeting to another, from one conference call to another, from one task to another, and from one conversation to another. Those busy workdays helped me keep my mind off my reality at home. But, with any pause or slowdown of work, the sadness always returned heavily like a wave engulfing me.

I fought hard to have the energy to complete necessary housework within the home. After work, I just wanted to lay around or sleep. I was learning about the rollercoaster of emotions involved with grief. Grief is a beast! The fight to overcome takes all your human strength.

The morning of July 21st, 2011, I recall crying out during my commute to work, "Jake, I really miss you and need to see one of your signs today!" I drove to work just thinking about him. I asked God to let me know Jake was okay. It was so important for me to know Jake was with Jesus. If I could imagine him being with Jesus, then I knew in my heart everything was alright. I was in a dark place and needed comfort.

As the workday was ending my co-worker, Tammy, stopped by my office. She told me she was going to be off work for a few days spending time with her grandchildren. During our conversation a strange motion caught my attention. I looked out the window and saw a huge spiraling and twisting funnel of what I believed was steam on the north side of the property. My first thoughts: this must be an underground water main rupture or a steam line rupture. However, upon further examination the location did not seem logical and the size of the spout was much too tall for a line rupture and we had no steam lines running underground. The spout spanned up into the sky as far as I could see from my second-floor office. Tammy left my office to investigate. She called me from her car. In amazement she said, "That was the biggest dust twister ("dirt devil") I have ever seen!" She said a truck driver had taken a photo of it on his flip phone and she would send it to me. I just sat back in my office chair and began to smile. I immediately knew Jake's love of the movie *Twister*. I recalled all the times we had watched the VHS tape with his eyes fixed on the screen, watching in awe of the power of the tornado. This was of no coincidence to me. I knew what I had prayed out of desperation that morning and now God was providing needed comfort. This "dirt devil" was specific to me and no one except Davy, myself, and close friends would grasp the connection. The event recharged my spirit. I was learning once again God reveals Himself in personal and unique ways. My heart was warm knowing God heard my prayer again. I could almost feel my heart smile. This event reinforced and reinvigorated prayer. He does listen! My prayer life began to transform. I was beginning to learn about the "Comforter" spoken of in John 14:16 KJV. I began a prayer journal and dug into the Bible wanting to learn as much as possible. I started faithfully and persistently reading devotionals to help me in my studies.

On Jake's birthday my friend, Rebecca, made me a homemade tornado-in-a-jar filled with blue glitter and a water solution. When she handed it to me it looked like a bottle of watery blue solution. I had no idea what was in the jar. But she said, "Shake it!" After shaking, a blue spiraling tornado formed in the jar. She knew Jake's love of tornadoes. And, she thought it would be something creative and special for a unique gift. Hunter loved the jar and shook it often. We placed it on a shelf with other figurine gifts from Jake's funeral. Another friend gave us a battery-operated tornado model and Hunter placed it on a shelf in his room. Hunter found it special he could share in some of his big brother's favorite things. It was a way of keeping Jake's memory alive. Though he is not with us, these positive memories offered us comfort.

"And I will pray the Father, and He shall give you

another Comforter, that He may abide with you for ever."

John 14:16 KJV

Rocky Point Principles:

God brings comfort in a unique way specific to the believer.

God is in control of all His creations.

Man places much faith in coincidence

failing to consider mathematical odds.

The Box

Living in the same home where Jake was raised since the age of 5 was painful. Each day I awoke to reminders of Jake surrounding me. Going to a busy and fast-paced work environment provided my mind a little therapy. After all, I was away from the pictures reminding me of his permanent absence. Family, friends, and community sent many keepsake gifts to the funeral and days following the funeral. We were overwhelmed with framed pictures, statues, and figurines. These lined almost every room of our home adding to the already existing memorabilia. Upon walking in the door after work I returned to all the constant cues. It's odd how memorabilia can bring you comfort but at the same time make you sad. His belongings were a reminder they would forever be without their owner. As a grieving mom, I could not turn loose of his possessions because they once belonged to Jake. However, I knew deep inside I could not stare at them daily. I remember a friend had given us some advice after Jake's passing. She said, "You will learn sometimes you have to put things in a box and only open the box when you are strong enough." I was learning just how true this was becoming in our grief journey. My body and my mind were still fresh to the tragedy. The surrounding memorabilia was turning our once vibrant home into a funeral home.

My mind was so overwhelmed I could not bring myself to relocate the items. Another grieving mother informed me it was eight years before she had the strength to go through her son's belongings. She instead closed the door and only entered his bedroom to clean and dust. The advice of putting things in a box and only opening the box when you are strong enough was being repeated to me. Fortunately, his room was located upstairs and was the only room on the second floor. The flood of memories and the daunting reminder of his absence all haunted that room. I could no longer go into his room. I was living a nightmare and some days I felt as though I might surely suffocate. The darkness and depression all seemed very hopeless. I continued sinking deeper and deeper by the day.

I was learning grief is an emotional beast. Why? Because grief is the only emotion known to man which contains all other emotions within it. Grief encapsulates anger, sadness, love, joy, sometimes peace, regret, shame, alienation, fear, disgust, anticipation, and hopelessness. There are minutes where you think about your loved one and warmth saturates the memories. When you have those good memories surface from time to time, you feel peace. Then, there are moments when you get angry over the events leading up to the death. There are moments where you regret your decisions. I live daily with the regret of allowing my son to go duck hunting. Or, at moments I get angry with relatives who fail to mention his name. I get angry with those who never recognize the anniversary of his death or his birthday. He was important to me! I am now in a different place and can better understand the anniversary and birthday failures. People struggle to remember the birthdays and anniversaries of the living. However, there are still some triggers which occur. I strive to protect my emotions much better than I did in the days following his death.

Yes, grief is an emotional giant. It is a bad rollercoaster. Some days it is minute to minute changes in emotion. A trigger can come, and laughter comes to you about a funny memory. Then, another reminder comes in the same day and you are crying once again with salty tears on inflamed and irritated eyeballs which cried all night the prior night. Making plans in the height of grief is difficult. It is minute to minute and day to day. Every day I strived to progress and find new coping mechanisms. When you thought you had it figured out, then came another major setback. It was as if each time I took one step forward, I was taking two steps back. I could not conquer grief. For a person who liked to be in control, I could not master my emotions. I could not solve the grief rollercoaster!

And so, put it in a box and only open the box was my new approach. But, how could I get all these things packed into one room, shut the door, and only visit when I am strong?

Start Packing

Two years after losing Jake, Davy came home from work. He walked in the door and made an unexpected announcement: "Lori, I have found us a house and we are moving. I want you to go see it and I want us to contact a realtor to show us the house. Mom is friends with Mary Lou who is a realtor and she will arrange to show us the house." He went on to explain, "We are prisoners in our very own home, and we have to move from here." His persistence was difficult to receive. However, I knew deep down what he was saying was all very true. I was not only hesitant because of our memories in the Mountain Ridge Road home, but also because the new home he had selected was, in my opinion, much too large for just the three of us. The prospective home, only 7 minutes away on Spence Chapel Road, was five bedrooms and over 4,000 sq. ft under roof. Attractive to Davy's wishes was the 18.5 acres in a private and serene location. I could not deny the positive points. It truly was a picture-perfect location, only 7 minutes from town, but still very rural and private. Reluctantly, I looked at the home several times. Each time I went to tour the home and the property, I became a little more attached to it, and a little more detached from our Mountain Ridge home. I began to see myself living there, drinking coffee on the porch abounding with southern charm, swinging on the porch swing or sitting in a rocker overlooking the countryside. I started to imagine cooking all those meals in the kitchen and serving them in the formal dining room. I began to see myself decorating every square inch of the three levels making my new nest. Shockingly, I could see myself beginning to entertain guests in our home. For two years I had found myself no longer able to open our home for overnight guests. The grief had consumed my physical energy and my mental focus. We continued to gather with the other families impacted by the tragedy and a few close friends to try to laugh and uphold one another. However, the idea of inviting out of town family or friends in for an overnight stay was overwhelming. The mere thought crippled me mentally. I was subconsciously aware remaining on Mountain Ridge Road was delaying my healing. It was changing me day by day. The longing for the life we lived before the tragedy was like quicksand to my heart and soul.

The Move

In March of 2011, we signed the papers and received the keys to our new home. This new step required quite a purge—a conscious decision of what to take, what to donate, and what to toss. The weight of every decision for each item felt as if it might bring me to my knees. It was almost like choosing which limb of your body to amputate. But, little by little and box by box each room was packed. It's no wonder the task of moving is such an emotional one! With only two years under my belt of being a grieving mom, my heart grew weaker and weaker by the day because of missing Jake. I was working full-time plus overtime. The added stress of the move felt as if it could be my breaking point.

Working in management was more than a full-time job. I had to work many hours to meet the minimum requirements for leadership. Leaders pack a heavy weight on their shoulders, and it is "24-7". The scope of their vision is broader. Their decisions are far-reaching. Their mission is broad. A leader does not look at tomorrow. They look at next year. And the farther up the career ladder, the further out your vision must be able to concentrate. Upper management functions take energy and unrivaled focus. I recall one day while I was at work Davy went through the things in Jake's bedroom and began boxing his items. I recall us crying over the phone together. His room was the last to be packed. Davy was brave to be able to go through Jake's possessions piece by piece. But he knew it must be done before we could begin to remodel and place the Mountain Ridge home on the market.

I pleaded with Davy, "I still need a room in our new home which is Jake's." I promised to only put his bed, his furniture, and his trophies. All of Jake's clothing was donated to friends and to charities except for two of his school jackets embroidered with his name and a few items which we saved for Hunter. My sister had two special keepsake quilts made from Jake's shirts. Each block of that t-shirt quilt had a special story or a memorable story behind it. I was placing one foot in front of the other and I knew today's struggle to get through the move would help the entire family move forward. Some days I felt like I was going to suffocate in my grief. Turning loose of the home where Jake was raised removed the bandage off my wounds and poured salt into them.

We settled into the new home and I found therapy in nesting and making a new home for the three of us. Unpacking was therapeutic. I was once again forced to dust off my organization skills and create a new beginning for us. The grief continued, but I could feel I was engaging in new coping skills. The broken heart was there and the weary mind still present, but keeping it focused on establishing a new home gave me a new purpose.

When our belongings were moved out of the Mountain Ridge home, my in-laws repainted all the interior walls. A contractor updated the flooring. Room by room the old home was remodeled. The more the old home was remodeled the more I was able to detach mentally. It was placed on the market and sold quickly.

Following the move, I plunged deeper and deeper into my role in management bringing my work home with me each evening. I found work to be healing because I was forced to refocus my attention. However, I was finding my mental exhaustion was at an all-time high. Once again, I began sinking deeper and deeper. I was waking up more tired than when I went to bed. I was weak. It began to affect my physical health. I had received a couple of bad reports from the doctor which all tied back to stress and lack of rest. My body was sick and now my immune system was beginning to attack my own body. My grief was snowballing and every mechanism I was reaching for was failing. The vacuum created by the loss was bringing me to a halt. What do I mean by vacuum? There was a sweet, beautiful, and warm 17-year old boy who was satisfying my soul. And, then in an instant, he was no longer there. Our family was no longer complete. When he was plucked away the vacuum in my soul needed him back. My heart was longing for something to fill this void. The vacuum was not filled by moving into a new home. The relief of moving in was only temporary. The vacuum could not be filled by working more hours. The depression and grief were consuming. The things I tried were not working. They were only temporary. During my depression and grief, Davy was turning to alcohol to fill his vacuum. His turning to alcohol brought on added tension to our life.

I once again started to read my Bible with a new and very different dedication. I was digging in my Bible searching for answers daily like a person with a treasure map and a shovel. The more I read, the more I found. The more I found, the more I wanted to find. The more I found the more I wanted to share with someone else. The more I shared with someone else, the more energized I became to find more. The words were coming alive. I was finding out why Jesus is referred to as the Living Water. I was discovering a new thirst inside me for God's Holy Word and for deeper and deeper understanding. The Holy Scripture was speaking directly to me. I found myself totally addicted to the Bible. I began to pray with a new passion. The more I read in the Holy Bible the more I understood ways to pray and ask for healing. Each time I opened the Bible it taught me new ways to pray.

My long drive to work was a perfect opportunity for me to turn my car into a mobile moving sanctuary. I was all alone in the car. I could speak out loud to God and no one would interfere. I could cry out loud to God and no one could hear. I began speaking to Him with a new attitude asking for His daily help in my broken heart. Soon after, I was drawn to listen to Christian worship music during my drive and I noticed something was coming alive inside me. I was changing. The words to the music were all filled with meaning. I was identifying with the lyrics. It was like I could feel each word in every lyric. I could now identify the lyrics to the scripture I had been reading. It was piercing my heart. Something new was awakening inside me craving a deeper walk with the Lord. Each morning before work I dusted off my Bible and made a conscious decision to dig deeper into Scriptures looking for direction from God. I began to set my alarm earlier and earlier striving for more time before work to study for His direction. I returned to church and began serving in children's ministry. Hunter attended with me.

<u>Rocky Point Principle:</u>

God's Word is alive to the believer.

The Trophies

I prepared the house for my brother and his wife to visit us from Oklahoma for Thanksgiving. They were going to stay in the room I still referred to as Jake's room. I had to enter the room and begin dusting and cleaning. Walking in the door of the room brought a rush of emotions. There were two solid oak bookshelves filled with framed pictures, memorabilia collections, basketball trophies, football trophies, and a few autographed photographs.

The room is difficult to enter. It is not difficult to look at the memories. It is not difficult to touch or handle the memorabilia and personal belongings. All those memories are embedded in my heart and in my mind, but they evoke an emotion where I long to see Jake make new memories with his family. By just opening and walking into the room you miss his very presence. You miss his kiss, his voice, his touch, his laughter. You miss what made up his life-- liveliness!

As I reached into the two oak bookshelves and began to dust all the pictures and their frames, the trophies, the memorabilia, I picked up the first-place pinewood derby trophy he won while participating in *Boy Scouts*. I reminisced of the time and the joy we had making the pinewood derby car. I had glued the weights on the car myself to attempt to put mass in the front of the car to make it travel down the track fast. Much to our amazement, his car was undefeated that day. I remember the smile on his face as he won each of those races.

I looked at all the football and basketball trophies. I recalled the time we spent and the gas we burned up as we traveled to practices, games, and tournaments. Some tournaments were on the other end of the state. We had good times at all those events. Friends and families spent a lot of time watching the children playing sports. I remember the stress involved--the bad calls, the constant rearrangement of the schedules to attend the events, the housework which awaited your return, the piles of laundry no one had time to finish because of always being on the go. During the busy times of life, we were forced to live out of a laundry basket because we were always "on the go".

While dusting his trophies a heavy sadness came over me. I said, "Jake, you didn't take any of these trophies with you. You left them for me to dust!". With our priorities being placed on career and sporting events God had been our last priority. This turned into a moment of deep regret and shame. Oh, how I wished I could turn back time and restart! When Jake died my mind immediately questioned whether he was with Jesus. How do I know he is in heaven? Then suddenly, relief came with the memory of Jake getting saved at Trace Creek's Vacation Bible School when he was 11 years old. He was invited to attend VBS by a neighbor friend who I am thankful saw the greater spiritual need in Jake's life. When tragedy happens among our first questions is heaven. It is a question every human will face in their lifetime. When Jake died, I needed to know he was in heaven. I only wished I had such a great concern for his spiritual state prior to his passing. If only I could go back in time and do things differently. While examining those trophies I began to feel deep repentance for the priorities I had placed in front of loving and serving God with all my heart. Chasing after earth's trophies will bring only temporary contentment. I should have been chasing after a relationship with my Creator.

Do not lay for yourselves treasures on earth, where moth and rust destroy and where thieves break in and steal; But lay up for yourselves treasures in heaven, where neither moth nor rust destroys and where thieves do not break in and steal. For where your treasure is, there your heart will be also. Matthew 6:19-21 (NKJV)

God wants us to set our heart on Him, not on earthly trophies we can't take with us. He is our contentment. We will leave this world with nothing but our faith in God.

I challenge you to reach Matthew 6:19-21 again. To paraphrase in my own words, "Show me where your prized possessions are, and I will show you where your heart is!"

Rocky Point Principle:

The greatest gift a parent can give their child is to
nurture them in the things of God.

A Knock at the Door

Our small town of Mayfield built a bypass which extends around the town to allow travelers to avoid the downtown area. Driving to work and taking shortcuts to make my way to the local grocery and retail stores, I had always noticed the bright blue illuminated sign displaying directions to the local Chief Cornerstone Church. The sign is located next to a telephone pole at the intersection of the Highway 121 bypass and highway 464 (Backusburg Road). As normally, I made last-minute trips to town for errands. Those trips often occurred in the evenings. The sign was viewable from long distances on the bypass (as the bypass is not busy with other signs or hints of industry). The glowing blue sign with a large white arrow points in the direction of the church. I have driven past this sign hundreds of times as I made my trips to town.

One Sunday morning while sitting in the balcony at Trace Creek Church, sitting ever so snuggly and close to my son, Hunter, as he drew on a notebook, sketching motorcycles and action figures, I listened to church announcements. While occasionally glancing down at Hunter's artwork, our pastor announced the community had churches struggling. He explained the county had churches "splitting", churches without pastors, and he asked for the church to pray for those situations. He announced one of the members, Bro. Keith, had been called to become the Pastor of Chief Cornerstone. This was a church which had closed but reopened in July 2009. He described how our church would help support Chief Cornerstone to give them a good start. Support doesn't always mean financial. Often it means, providing experience and knowledge through people. He explained that a few of our members had been called to go and help Cornerstone in their ministry launch.

I drove approximately 27 miles to work each day and would get very bored with the same old trip so on some days I opted to discover new roads to and from work. I love finding new routes and enjoy the drive of the backroads, discovering new locations. On this day I took a different route, a road (Highway 1710) which is very rural, very curvy, and can be quite dangerous in the evenings. I traveled the curves and hills. Rounding the curve, I looked to the north and noticed Chief Cornerstone Church topping the hill. Connecting the sight of the building with what I had recently heard at church regarding their launch, I stuck out my hand toward my window and said aloud, "God, bless that church and bring them people". My quiet time in the car each morning, as I traveled for 30 minutes daily, was my time to hold a conversation with myself and the Lord. My quiet drives became a vehicle for continued healing. My car was my sacred sanctuary.

I grew to like this new route to work. So, when bored with the bypass, I would opt to travel Old Golo Road and Backusburg to my destination. Each time I would pass the church I would ask God to bless the church. There was a special interest in that church on the hill each time I passed it. I could almost feel a tug on my heart. This was such a strange feeling. During my commute, it was almost as if I traveled so I could see the church---very odd and highly unexplainable for me. At times I thought God had placed a special prayer burden on my heart for this new church.

On a Saturday, I heard a knock at the door. Upon opening the door, much to my surprise, it was Bro. Keith. He stated jokingly, "I knew exactly where you lived". (Bro. Keith's brother built and formerly lived in the home we purchased on Spence Chapel Road.) He smiled as he handed me a piece of paper which was a flyer for Chief Cornerstone's upcoming Homecoming service. He said, "We would love for you to come and visit. Our Homecoming service is tomorrow." I took note of his friendly smile and his enthusiasm. This was more than a coincidence to me. I had been praying for the Church. I was in the audience when their ministry launch was announced. The sign had been grabbing my attention every time I passed by it. And now, the Church's new pastor appears at my door "out of the blue"!

I laid the flyer on my kitchen island. I was cleaning the house and each time I passed through the kitchen I looked down at the paper and then finally said to myself, "I am going to visit this church tomorrow". I knew there was an unexplainable draw to this church.

On that Sunday morning, my sister and Hunter joined me as we attended the morning worship at Chief Cornerstone. Davy was away on a hunting trip to Colorado. Upon entering the church, I immediately noticed the friendly faces surrounding me. Everyone was walking around shaking hands and acknowledging the people, no matter where they sat, no matter where they stood. This was very neat to see a church planted in the middle of a cow pasture being so friendly with everyone. The worship service was moving. Hunter, who was terrified of crowds, looked around as he noted two other friends from school. He smiled and waved as he noted friends in the audience. Finally, when Bro. Keith stood at the pulpit to present the sermon I hung on every single word. I was amazed to look across the sanctuary and note another family who had recently lost their daughter. I found after losing Jake, I take note and think often of those parents who have lost their children. I think about them and wonder if they feel the way I do, and if they have experienced the closeness to God I have experienced. While listening to Bro. Keith and enjoying the sermon, I looked up and noted another couple of parents we have known for years, who lost their son in a car accident. I had not seen them in years but related to them in their tragic loss. Was this yet another sign? I couldn't help but take note of this! I was feeling drawn to this Church and I could not wait to come back! I could not wait for Davy to experience the service as soon as he was home from Colorado.

I felt a pull inside me. I began to feel myself disconnecting from my management career. It was as if each day became a little harder than the previous day to be a manager. I was losing the passion I once had for the position. I began to pray out of desperation for God to open a new door for me. Much to my surprise within 48 hours, an opportunity in my new church was identified. After praying for several days, I notified my superior of my intent to resign. I was suffering burn out. It was time to find healing. It was time to take a new position where I could make my family a high priority. The position at the church was a short drive of six miles from our home. The flexibility of raising Hunter and being able to drive him to and from school delivered immediate peace.

My very first day on the job a flock of geese flew overhead. I closed my eyes and breathed in a real deep breath as I listened to them fly over while honking. The sight and sound of the geese always comforted me and brought me to a place where I would stop and lift my head toward the sky, then close my eyes and sigh. I knew immediately this was a sign of confirmation I was making the right move. I immediately began to find something remarkably rewarding about the work. It seemed as if God was always placing people in my path for me to assist. I found this to be very satisfying and reassuring of my decision. I had left a career of daily monotony and was experiencing a spiritual reward for helping others.

Somehow, even though I was weak, I still had the ability to share with others what I had learned through our tragedy. I was discovering as strangely as it may sound helping others gave my soul a burst of spiritual adrenaline. And, I was discovering that each morning's study in the Word of God oddly enough was being used during the day or thereafter. It was like God was preparing me each morning through my Bible studies. How on earth is He so foretelling? I was learning His wisdom is always preparing us for what is ahead. My faith was growing and expanding. I was truly learning more and more about His greatness.

In 2012 Davy stopped drinking. He began to follow Christ, attending church of his own free will without being asked. Shortly after, our precious Hunter accepted Jesus Christ's gift of grace and was baptized. Then, Davy and I made the decision to be baptized together. God has created a beautiful marriage and family life centered around Christ's kingdom.

When I decided to follow Christ, there were friendships I left behind. To be honest, I left them behind because there was a lot of drinking involved. I could feel my spirit disconnecting from the drinking. In my inner spirit I felt shame being in the presence of the partying. (The seed of the Spirit is a strong seed. Once it is implanted in your heart things begin to change within you. Your desires change little by little and day by day.)[7] When I walked away, I had special peace about it. However, my heart grieved for the loss of togetherness with our close friends. What was amazing to me is one of the most endearing friendships I walked away from was restored on September 29th when the friends walked into our church. I look back at the date (Jake's birthday) and I think to myself, "What an amazing God! He knew I grieved for the special friendship and He would give me my heart's desire! And, He would do it on a special date to celebrate my obedience to Him." Our friends attend church faithfully and God has uprooted their old lifestyle and given them new life and new purpose. They are fulfilled and at peace. The change in their life has spread to others within their sphere of influence. They now serve to grow Christ's kingdom in various ministries and outreaches. We are honored to serve beside them. How great is our God!

Over the years since following Christ, God has blessed us with more friends than we ever had before following Him. Honestly, I can't count my friends! They are my sisters and brothers united in Christ!

Rocky Point Principles:

The seed of the Holy Spirit is a strong
seed changing the desires of the heart.

God surprises you on special dates
letting you know He is in control.

As I began to grow in Bible knowledge and become closer to the Lord, I began to ask God to change Davy's mind about our Spence Chapel Road home. In my prayer time, I told God I was overwhelmed because I spent my time off from work cleaning the home. The new home was three levels of carpet floors with the only tile in kitchen, utility, and bathroom areas. I worked, attended three church services weekly, taught Sunday School, and served in the women's jail ministry. I longed to serve God more and more. I had a strong desire inside me to become more involved in ministry. I was asking God for more time to serve Him and His people without all the cleaning requirements of this home. The home became more of a "ball and chain". What was therapeutic to me in March of 2011 had now become a source of exhaustion. That may sound silly to some, but the house had become quite a burden to me. I was ready to downsize! The home began to develop a list of maintenance items requiring attention. I remember kneeling down in my prayer room of the basement one morning and praying, "Father, I don't know how you can change Davy's mind about this home. He loves the property so much. He loves the location and it is a perfect location. But, Father, the house is a 'ball and chain' to me because of the size and because of the things which are wrong with the house, like carpeting, Father. I need hardwood floors which are easy to maintain." (Davy has a love for thick carpet!) I began little by little to pour my heart out to Him telling Him my heart's desires in a home. I asked Him for a home which was energy efficient and easy to maintain. I recall explaining to Him the problem with water entering the basement during heavy rains and the high electric bills. I felt guilty for praying this prayer. I felt filled with shame for asking for something which others might find selfish. But my heart's desire was to be able to spend more time serving God and less time cleaning a home which was much too large for the three of us.

On Tuesday, May 10th, 2016 it was a normal day. The normal routine morning: take Hunter to school, go to work, prioritize the list of the day's tasks and then begin completing them one by one. That afternoon as I was working at my desk, I received a voice-activated mobile alert on my cell phone: "Tornado warning for your area". My co-worker opened the door and we began to look outside. We looked to the west and saw a large grouping of immense thick clouds, but we saw no evidence of a defined tornado spout. Davy was working 12-hr night shift, so I wanted to make sure he was awake to watch for storms. I called him. Thankfully, he answered. I said to him, "Hey, I was just making sure you are awake because there is a tornado warning for Mayfield." He responded with "Lori, it is so bad here. It's almost as if the thunder will not stop. It is a constant rumble. It is bad." The phone went dead. I called him back and received the "all circuits are busy" message. My heart began to race, and I ran back outside to look at the sky looking for signs of a tornado. I was growing anxious and nervous. My co-worker, Lisa, was outside videoing the large storm moving across the field with her cell phone. And I said with great fear, "Lisa, that looks like it is headed straight for my house! I have to leave now!" I left driving over the speed limit rushing to get home. I continued to try to contact Davy repeatedly. Within only 3 miles from my home I received a text message from Davy stating, "the house, the shop, everything is gone." My fears had become reality. I continued trying to get a voice call out on my phone to speak to him, but I could not reach him. As I approached my community, I struggled to get vehicles of on-lookers out of my way on Spence Chapel Road. I could not get home quick enough. The closer I got to our property the more I saw scattered debris. I saw pieces of bent and torn tin metal scattered in the fields. I pulled into our very long driveway while noticing all the downed trees laying across the limestone gravel path. I was forced to drive in the yard and make my way to our home maneuvering around fallen trees and pieces of littered housing materials. As I looked on top of the hill my eyes navigated to the location of our home, and there I saw a beaten and tethered house opened to the atmosphere. As I drove into the driveway I immediately cried out, "God, why did you have to answer my prayer in this manner? Why God? Why? Why this way?"

The top floor where Jake and Hunter's rooms were located was peeled back and I noticed some remaining and recognizable pieces of furnishings scattered. Hunter's bed mattress folded in half and littered with various parts of the home on top of it. My eye scanned the property as I tried to process the destruction. It was not a nightmare. This was real! This tattered battlefield was our former beautiful property.

Only one wall of our shop remained. No signs were left of the machine shed and another garden tool shed. The bright orange tractor sat in the middle of the field as the machine shed which housed it had been sucked completely away. As I scanned the devastation of our property my eyes thankfully spotted Davy sitting on the tailgate of his storm-weathered Ford truck crying and shaking his head. I ran to him, hugging him. I was so grateful he was alive and unharmed. He began telling me after the phone died, he went to the front porch and discovered the tornado coming across the field headed straight toward our home. He ran back inside the house and ran to the basement. As he reached the third step making his way down the stairs, the house started to break away. He felt the storm's vacuum begin to pull at his uniform work shirt. He heard the horrific sound of boards breaking, glass shattering, as he ran to safety. He prayed out loud, "God, in a few minutes I will either be with You and Jake or I will be with my wife in about 10 minutes! Either is fine, Lord." He saw large sheets of tin metal flying in front of the French doors of the walk-out basement. He was afraid the house would collapse on the basement and he would be trapped. In panic, he stayed away from the glass doors. But he was too afraid to enter the guest room which was in the southeast corner of the basement for fear of entrapment. He ran back and forth between a downstairs den and a basement hall area. While holding his head between his hands he repeatedly explained to me, "The sound of your house breaking apart is one you will never forget!".

Emergency management and neighbors began appearing one by one and filling up our long driveway. Friends, family, and church family arrived and began boxing up items. The church began coordinating equipment, various types of assistance, boxes, storage trailers, storage locations and helping with clean up. Looking at the cleanup it was overwhelming. It was hard to imagine the property would be normal again. Our thoughts and concerns had to be focused on the rainstorms coming. We had to rush to get all remaining items into dry storage locations.

I spotted a long-time friend, Leta, who I had not seen in years walking up the long driveway to our storm-damaged home carrying a Graves County Eagle sport's jacket. She was smiling saying, "Look what we found! My mom and dad's chicken barns were destroyed by the tornado. As we were cleaning up the debris, we saw your son's jacket lying on the ground. I saw the name on the jacket and knew this jacket belonged to you. I just had to stop and bring it to you right away!" I was brought to a halt trying to process the odds of Jake's jacket being found. Her parent's property is 1.6 miles across the field or 2.5 miles traveling by car. And what was even more unbelievable? The jacket was untouched by the tornado's wrath. The jacket ended up at her parent's property located at 929 Crowder Road. 9/29 is Jake's birthday. Mentally, I try to process the odds of such an occurrence. Even through the storms of life God is present and lets you know by His thumbprints He is there and with you.

A friend crawled up into a tree in our backyard and pulled down the other school letter jacket of Jake's. It was completely clean. No dirt, no stains. Perfect! Wow! All of Jake's trophies were taken away by the wrath of the storm. The pinewood derby car and trophy were also gone. I have those memories tucked away in my heart.

A tornado is such a powerful force, spinning and traveling where it desires, lifting and carrying items for miles upon miles or just feet if it so desires. It cuts a wide path of destruction. And the amazement of this force is this: a few feet from the path items can seem to be placed in safety untouched and unharmed. It picks and chooses destruction within its path. The path... unpredictable.

Rocky Point Principles:

Even through the storms of life, God
leaves traces of His thumbprints.

Man places much faith in coincidence
failing to consider mathematical odds.

Everything you see with your eyes can be lost.
Only that which is unseen, your faith, cannot be taken.

The Rebuild

Following the tornado of May 10, 2016, our home church and area churches once again became a lifeline to us throughout the cleanup process. History would repeat itself with the church surrounding us with love, support, and volunteer labor. The repetition of events reinforced the church as a beacon of light for the hurting, the broken, and those in need of rescue. In my spirit I believed God was redefining my flawed ideas of the church. The church was surrounding us to come to our aid. The body of Christ (the Church) was displaying life to me. The church is not dead, but alive. The blood is pumping and flowing through the body of Christ and it was moving my heart to have a deeper and deeper loyalty. Another couple from church, Tommy and Lisa, who had also lost their son offered us a temporary home only 1.5 miles away. The home was conveniently located so we could work each night at the construction site. We were without a home for one night.

The insurance company sent an engineer to the home and immediately deemed it uninhabitable authorizing full demolition. Now, we could focus on moving forward. We began to pray for the right contractor to rebuild our home. We asked for a contractor who had our best interest at heart.

A church friend took vacation time and operated an excavator to demolish the home. I recall watching the first sweep of the excavator's bucket striking the home and the sad feeling which developed. I knew I had to drive away. I couldn't bear to watch the clearing away of the remainder of the home. The excavator operator picked up a steel beam which supported the suspended concrete patio and tossed it to the ground. The steel beam stood up and landed right in the center of the septic tank, rupturing the septic tank. Once we were further along, we would need to dig up the old one and replace with a new one. Every day was a bad day with more bad news. I could not see a future. It felt as if this was going to be never-ending! I knew God had answered my prayer about the house's maintenance issues and my need to downsize. But I was struggling with trust as we continued to suffer additional losses.

Within a few days the home was demolished down to the foundation. We were making plans to rebuild back on the same foundation and basement. However, we would eliminate a level.

I knew God had answered my prayer changing Davy's heart about the home, but I was still questioning Him about why the degree of devastation. I continued, however, to dig deeper into Scripture and forced myself to stay focused. I was learning a whole new trust in my relationship with God.

It was good for us to stay in a home nearby. Each evening we worked on debris cleanup preparing the site for a contractor to be able to start his work in August. God had blessed us during a time of desperate need. Davy was working 12-hour swing shift. He spent all his available time at the cleanup site. I worked during the day, ate supper, and then each evening I worked on the demolition of the basement.

We took off one weekend to get away from the stress driving 2.5 hours to Nashville to spend the night and look for kitchen design materials. We thought it would be good for our minds to focus on a "go forward" instead of staying focused on the debris cleanup. While we were away another storm came and blew our mailbox out into the roadway. A neighbor notified us our mailbox was down. Davy and I both looked at each other and I recall him saying, "the one thing the storm did not get was our mailbox and now it too has been torn down." And we painfully laughed. We notified a friend and asked if he would get the mailbox put back up so we could receive mail. Our friend discovered that the storm had blown a section of tarp off our subfloor and the basement was full of water. Therefore, we lost the interior basement walls we had worked so diligently to salvage.

In August construction began with a new subfloor due to the record rainfall which had occurred since the May tornado. Then walls began to be erected on the home's main floor. At the same time, Davy and I were working to tear out each piece of sheetrock and mineral popular walls in the basement's "man cave". Nail by nail and board by board, carpet strip by carpet strip, everything was removed down to the bare concrete basement walls.

As we were building the home, an expensive new stainless submersible pump had to be installed. The next week a discovery was made that the gas lines were stretched when the propane tank was moved by the storm and now new gas lines would have to be run from the tank to the home. Even stuff underground and protected from the elements had been affected! How could this be? Everything was going wrong! I would cry out often, "Why God, Why? I just don't understand!" It is one thing after another, struggle after struggle, hurt after hurt, tragedy followed by material loss. Why God? Why? I just don't understand. Is this a punishment? Why are others around me so blessed? Why do they not have the losses, the heartbreak, the gaping wound of losing their child? Why? God? Why? Even after I began following You, God, I am still on the losing end? Why? I could only see what we had lost. I still was having trouble trusting. I found it impossible to envision being back in a home.

This tornado and the mounting losses which followed reopened wounds of grief in a very bad way. I was suffering with questions. Once again, I found myself hopeless. I returned to some early childhood thoughts of how God is waiting to punish me for all my wrongdoing. From a small child and into my youth, I suffered a series of noticeable patterns. When I tried to make a conscientious effort to get close to God very bad things would happen. My homelife was toxic from childhood. I related those bad things occurring to me in a punishing way. I blamed God. And, I developed an attitude, "God doesn't like me!". It was very real to me. I could only see God as the punisher. My homelife reinforced this ideology. These thoughts welled up inside me and fueled a misguided heart of unhealthy fear toward Him. And, I ran for years from Him. I had run for 39 years and now I was questioning Him. But there was something on the inside taking me back to day 44 of the Rocky Point search where I surrendered my life to Him and then He responded the next day with Jake's discovery. To be honest, I was a confused and tired mess! My mind was pulled in one direction, and my heart was being pulled in another.

As the house was under construction numerous heavy trucks hauled building materials over a concrete bridge to our property. The long driveway crossed over a creek and the only way to enter the driveway to bring in construction materials was to cross the concrete bridge which was poured over a large metal culvert. Additional dirt had to be hauled in because our topsoil was lost during the debris cleanup. The soil was littered with nails, screws, shards of broken glass, and shattered tile. As we pulled in the driveway in the evening the car headlights would illuminate the shards of broken glass giving a disco ball surface effect. The dirt was later scraped up with a tractor bucket to clear away the debris.

As one of the dump trucks entered, the concrete bridge collapsed and broke into three sections. Our bridge, the sole entry to our property, was gone! It was the only way for construction to continue. Davy called me to report what had occurred. I recall telling him, "I can't take any more bad news, Davy. I just can't take anymore. It's never going to end!" It felt as if we would never be able to get our home finished.

I sat down and began to cry and sob. Then a moment of stillness came. I recalled something which had occurred before the tornado hit. The recollection of memories came like a flood to me. A few weeks before the tornado I had studied a devotional where Jesus predicted Peter's denial of Him in Luke 22:31-32 KJV. *"And the Lord said, Simon, Simon, behold, Satan hath desired to have you, that he may sift you as wheat; But I have prayed for thee, that thy faith fail not; and when thou art converted, strengthen thy brethren."* I recalled these same verses were on the radio when I was getting ready the same morning. Then, I went to church and my pastor had preached on the same verses describing the way wheat is sifted. The good grain is separated from the chaff. The chaff is the bad part. The grain is the part which is useful. There is a physical separation occurring as the wheat is prepared for its use. It was all being repeated to me. The same week I get in the car, turn on the radio to a Christian radio station and the same verses were being quoted by Evangelist Luis Palau. It felt as if these verses were following me around. I recall thinking "Ok, God. I am listening. I just don't know if you are showing me these verses repeatedly for myself or for someone else." (There are over 31,000 verses in the Holy Bible[8] so when verses are being repeated to you it is of no coincidence.) The odds are too rare to make all these things come together and unfold within such close timing. I was finally processing it all. These verses were in fact intended for me. Satan was desiring to sift us as wheat. I now realized God had been preparing me for what He knew we would face. I could now look at the loss and see it in a different perspective.

I began to open the Bible and go back over the verses once again. The devil was sifting us like wheat. He was trying to shake us and destroy us, but I was encouraged how Jesus prayed for Simon Peter that his faith would not fail.

My faith was restored immediately upon the meditation of these Holy Scriptures. God has all of this under His control. He was warning me even before the tornado came. I was learning that He is a very good teacher if we pay attention and listen. It amazes me how when God answered my prayer for a low maintenance home the devil quickly swooped in to try to steal my joy and try to make me doubt my faith. As oddly as it might seem to some, Jesus words spoken to Peter were making even more sense in my current battlefield mess.

I prayed and dug deeper into Scripture, pouring out my heart and soul to the Lord. I realized He was growing my faith. He was asking me for a deeper trust. I had been taken on a hard detour in the storms of life, but I had assurance through Scripture I would be alright. I began to see how God was making all things new for us and preparing us for a better future. He was giving us a new bridge to the property, a new well, a new septic tank, a new set of gas lines to the home, a brand-new home, and a brand-new shop. I began to feel a whole new energy surfacing within me. God was truly in charge and together we would overcome all of this. Trust! I was learning what trust really meant. I was also learning how God teaches through repetition.

It was amazing how God always seemed to provide what we needed when we needed it. I certainly learned of His divine timing on Rocky Point. Now, I was learning He seems to show up in what appears to us as the final hour to meet our needs. He met every financial need and always on time!

We invited close friends to our property, and we stood on the cleared foundation of the home and held prayer over the future home and property. Our pastor prayed for a home built in record time, a home which was well built, a home which would glorify Him, and a home which would never again be devastated by storms or any other element. We all formed a circle and dedicated the foundation to the Lord. Walls were framed and went up one by one. Trusses were delivered. Right as the truss truck arrived the flock of geese flew over the building site and gave Davy and me a pause and a gentle smile. We could not wait for the roof to be completed with shingles to protect the interior. As soon as the roof was completed, we began writing Holy Scripture on studs with a permanent marker. Friends came and added additional scripture to the studs. This home was being dedicated to the Lord in every way. I think about all the additional contractors who came through the home: the electricians, the insulators, the sheetrock finishers, the painters. They saw the scripture as the home was being brought to completion. The home went up in record time with construction beginning in August and the home completed and ready for moving in two days before Christmas. Wow! What a great Christmas present to the three of us. Today, we live in the home and we call it our "divine downsize". The downsize: 1,576 sq. feet less than the original home! It is the perfect size for the three of us. God provided us an energy-efficient home. It is low maintenance. And, it has hardwood floors. Wink! Wink! Yes, He cares about our heart's desires. It is the home which the Lord built with His plans and with His timing. And while the devil tried to steal our joy when the tornado came, God had a much bigger plan. He would take the bad and turn it to the good. He had a plan the human eye could not see. He overcame Satan and all his tricks and schemes. What Satan used to harm, God was fore-knowing (all knowledgeable of past, present, and future) and I imagine He probably smirked at the enemy and his schemes.

God would demonstrate a lesson to us: Whatever we surrender to Him, He will repair. Whatever we refuse to surrender to Him, He cannot repair. Why? Because in the end God gets the glory. So, if we can claim man fixed our problems, then God is not glorified. When we know that God is the only One who could have fixed our situation, then He gets all the glory. And, God is all about glory because He is glory!

I hope as you read this story you noticed the date May 10, 2016. Yes, it is so difficult for the mind to comprehend. It is so beyond real for the mind to grasp that May 10, 2016, is the 20-year anniversary of the release of the movie, *Twister*.[9] And, the Mayfield tornado would strike on a specific date. Truly, God shows us in many ways He is in control. He leaves His thumbprints perfectly placed. My son's favorite movie and the memories we shared watching that movie over and over! And then I lift my head toward the sky, close my eyes, pause, take a deep breath, and feel the kiss of God upon my head. God is truly working and drawing us with His great and all-powerful love if only we will open our eyes and believe. God reminds us repeatedly He is very much in control of the universe. There is nothing which escapes His eyes. And there is nothing beyond His reach. And, He is a big God yet a very personal one for His believer.

<u>Rocky Point Principles:</u>

God is great at math.

There is no teacher like God.

A repetition of Bible verses is no

mere coincidence. Listen closely!

God is the first to be blamed and He is the last to be praised.

What we do not surrender to God will remain broken.

Thumbprints

As I look back at my journal entries, I thank God for His thumbprints. For instance, Debbie, my role model since middle school, was the one responsible for bringing Davy into my circle of friends. She tragically passed away. Her life and death made a profound impact on my life. I understand more in the present day the light which lived inside her. Today, I comprehend why she was different—the light dwelled within her. Her life, though very short, carried a depth of purpose and ministry. In the years to follow, Davy and I later dated and married. Then, I gave birth to Hunter on her birthday! Initially, we had forgotten Debbie was born on October 2nd. But one day Davy stopped to visit her tombstone. He made this shocking discovery of Hunter being born on her birthday. He called me from her grave to tell me the news. We both remarked of the odds of such an occurrence. Three hundred and sixty-five days in a year and yet Hunter was born on her birthday. He is a precious gift and his birthday is a humbling reminder of the sovereignty of God.

Our son, Jake's life ended tragically. In less than 24 hours after my heart's surrender to God, Jake and Mckenzie were recovered after an exhausting 45-day search. I exhausted the means of man to find healing from my grief and discovered God's nature and true ways. Even when we believe our life is in chaos and scattered pieces, God continues to be present. He remains a God of order. It is all within His sovereignty.

And now, who could possibly explain the tornado would come on the 20-year anniversary of Jake's most favorite movie of all time? I often find it difficult to explain to others in ordinary conversation without the recipient returning a blank pause. I have found those who don't have the light living inside them to have the hardest time processing God's nature and ways.

After the tornado, Jake's jacket would be found 1.6 miles away during debris cleanup at 929 Crowder Road (with Jake's birthday being 9/29). How about those mathematical odds? Try to calculate that on paper! This requires faith to understand such an occurrence. And, who could explain the way God chose to answer my prayer list regarding the home? I asked for him to change Davy's mind about the land and home. However, God heard my prayer and spared Davy's beloved location and took care of the home's laundry list of maintenance and size issues. He answered a list of my prayers in one event…only God! The thumbprints of God can only be seen when we look back at how God has woven our lives together ushering in various events. Our lives cross paths with people purposely. He knits everything together toward a greater purpose. I am solemnly and grievously aware only those tapped into a real relationship with God could ever comprehend His ways, His nature, and His timing. Yet, His ways are unmistakable and undeniable to the believer's eyes. Looking back across our lifespan, the God of this universe is a giant God overseeing it all. Nothing escapes His notice. Nothing takes Him by surprise. He chases and pursues a relationship with the lost. And, as I look back over the years, He was chasing relentlessly after my heart leaving thumbprints along the way. He had been drawing me to Him since I was a little girl. The events I had written off as mere coincidence were the thumbprints of a loving God.

Long ago the Lord said to Israel: "I have loved you, My people, with an everlasting love. With unfailing love I have drawn you to Myself." Jeremiah 31:3 NLT

The End of Your Rope

"You're blessed when you're at the end of your rope. With less of you
there is more of God and His rule. Matthew 5:3 (MSG)

As I look back over the years Jesus' great Sermon on the Mount speaks to
me in a very personal manner. I challenge you to stop now and read
Matthew chapter 5 and notice these things about Jesus' famous and well-
documented sermon:

1. Jesus climbed the mountaintop. He was not delivering His
    message from a valley.
2. Jesus climbed to the mountaintop before the Disciples. Again,
    notice "before the Disciples." There is no climb and certainly no
    pain of which Jesus is unfamiliar. In His climb to Golgotha, the
    horrible hill on which He was crucified, He experienced the
    ultimate pain and the most extreme torture.
3. The Disciples came to Him (Matthew 5:1 KJV). Those who
    desired to follow Him had to climb the mountain to be with Him.
    Climbing requires an effort. Climbing requires a decision to be
    made about whether we stay in the valley or we go to the
    mountaintop to be with Jesus.
4. The "multitudes" were in the valley. The multitude is the crowd.
    The crowd is the majority. The majority is the world.
5. Remaining in the valley takes no different activity. One just
    simply remains. Seeing the mountain and longing to be on top of it
    rather than remaining in the depression requires first seeking it out,
    then strategic steps to go to the top of the mountain.
6. The ones who were not willing to climb with Jesus remained in the
    valley. If one views the mountain from the valley you will remain
    in a vacuum (the place where desires and emotional strongholds
    have control.). Our desires are never truly quenched in the valley.
    Our thirst is never satisfied in the valley. There will always be
    spiritual discontentment in the valley. There will be a desire for
    the next best thing. It is a constant quest.
7. The Disciples listened to Him. "And He opened His mouth, and
    taught them, saying," (Matthew 5:2 KJV) Learning requires

listening. This is an area where we all struggle. The "...*prince of the power of the air...*" (aka the devil!) (Ephesians 2:2 KJV) strives diligently to keep you from listening. He keeps the airwaves full of distractions. It requires tuning out the cluttered airways and tuning into Jesus for peace.

8. Only a few climbed the mountain to be with Jesus. Again, the crowd remained in the valley. This verse makes me grieve but also lights a fire in the depths of my heart: *"Because strait is the gate, and narrow is the way, which leadeth unto life, and few there be that find it."* *(Matthew 7:14 KJV);* "For the gate is small and the way is narrow that leads to life, and there are few who find it." (NAS).

The "few who find it" are not the majority in the valley.

Jesus tells us that there will be few who accept Him. The few are those who followed up on the invitation of God calling them to Himself to follow His Son Jesus to the mountaintop. Jesus declares in John 6:44 (NKJV): *"No one can come to Me unless the Father who sent Me draws him; and I will raise him up at the last day."* On the difficult journey of loss, I found the lasting source of healing. I recognized the draw on my heart by My Father and freely accepted His Son's blood to cleanse me from the enormous sins of my past. I count on nothing but the blood of Jesus to cleanse me from my evil ways.

As I was flipping through channels one evening, I heard Christine Caine make a statement on the *TBN Channel,* "Jesus Christ saved my soul and the Word of God saved my mind." This quote resonates with me because it defines my healing in one sentence.

I am far enough along in my spiritual journey today to know this: I might not have discovered Jesus if there had not been an enormous vacuum inside me when I lost Jake. In my brokenness, I reached for the wrong things after losing him. I found out things, career, or busy activities do not satisfy the hurt and pain. When I began reaching daily for Jesus, I found my fullness, my wholeness, my peace, my joy, my laughter, my warmth, my purpose, my future, and my assurance of my eternal destiny. I found my Salvation, my Rescuer, My Redeemer in Jesus Christ. I found my contentment lies in Him and Him alone. There is no greater peace!

The horrible opposite to the "blessed" is the "cursed" and Jesus describes the "old me" in tragic depth. I readily identify my old self (before Jake's death) with these verses:

Luke 6:24-25 (NKJV) Jesus says *"But woe to you who are rich, for you have received your consolation. Woe to you who are full, for you shall hunger, woe to you who laugh now, for you shall mourn and weep."*

I think of my life in this manner: I was riding in the car with the radio blaring going 70 mph down life's road leading to the wide gate, but then tragedy came and spun me around. I then realized I was on the road to destruction (the wide gate to hell). The cursed are full. They are laughing not mourning. They are joyful not weeping. They are full, and they are satisfied by the world's feedings. They are consumed in the "all is well" moment. They are in the fast lane of life. I was in my consolation like Luke 6:24 (NKJV) describes. That consolation is a place of making you feel nice and comfortable while the rug is being pulled out from under your feet. It wasn't until I entered the vacuum state where a thing of great love was taken away that I began to reach for something to fill the vacuum and bring peace to my heart. I am thankful because of the prayers of the church I finally looked up and saw Jesus sitting at the top of the mountain. I decided to follow Him which requires effort—a choice must be made. That effort has made the journey beautiful and it has brought peace to my soul. I began to see God at work in many areas of my daily walk. It's been the best decision I have ever made in my life! If only I had made the choice sooner in my life…!

Whenever tragedy, catastrophe, hardship, or trials strike we decide: am I going to go through this with God or without God? We may not realize we are making a choice. During times of tragedy seeking God leads to answers. During times of tragedy failure to seek God leads to questions which only lead to more questions. These questions lead to a worn-down mental state and a state of hopelessness.

I cannot imagine having gone through devastation without Him. The vacuum is longing to be filled because it is empty. The vacuum must be filled. I tried to fill it with other things like a newer home. I tried to fill it with career, but that was exhausting both mentally and physically.

When I reached the end of my rope, I filled the vacuum with God. And God responded with grace and healing. Painfully, I have watched others fill their emptiness with alcohol, drugs, pills, food, people, relationships, things, hobbies, career, status, social media, games, sports, or wealth. The list is endless, and the enemy makes certain he adds more tools to his toolbox in this ever-changing fast-paced world.

Then said Jesus unto His disciples, *"If any man will come after Me, let him deny himself, and take up his cross, and follow Me"*. Matthew 16:24 KJV. The Cross has been heavy at times, but it has been victorious and filled with spiritual blessings not purchased with money. The material things leave you starving for the next best thing, the next generation of upgrades, the newer series or the newer technology, another drink, another pill, or the next fix. When I began to crave spiritual blessings, it was in those times I found something which satisfied my heart and well-being. I found out why His Bible offers the best feeding to satisfy our starved and deprived spirits. And, I have found prayer with Him brings continual reassurance of His work around me.

As I look back over His sermon in Matthew chapter 5, I know I would rather suffer persecution while serving my Jesus than laugh with the majority in the valley where I had formerly made a very comfortable home. Sure...the cross is heavy at times, but my relationship with Jesus is worth it all. Thank you for the vacuum which was created in my heart. Praise Jesus for His healing power. When I was at the end of my rope, He was ready to take over for me!

"You're blessed when you're at the end of your rope. With less of you there is more of God and His rule. Matthew 5:3 (MSG)

Rocky Point Principles:

What you reach for in the vacuum of despair

will determine your outcome.

When you are at the end of your rope

trust God to begin His work.

Be the "few" who find the narrow gate.

The key to overcoming emotional strongholds is the

daily climb to be alone with Jesus.

Understanding

Before 2009, I only knew the grief of a parent, aunts, uncles, cousins, school acquaintances, and one close friend. I state this not to minimize those losses. Every life is to be cherished. Every life is valuable. To further clarify every death was someone's child, no matter who they are and no matter how old they were at the time of death. So, I may help you to understand the very personal heart-wrenching pain and agony, I will do my best to explain this to you. When you lose a child a part of you dies. After all, our child was planned, and we anxiously awaited his delivery. He was the beautiful combination of a part of my body and my husband's body coming together and seeing God's miracle of life be born. We prepared for him in every way. As he grew inside me, I felt like I knew him even before he arrived in that hospital delivery room. We enjoyed each day watching him grow and develop. As new parents, we were excited about his first "goo", his first tooth, his first solid food, his turning over in the crib, his first steps and all the thrilling milestones of a child's development. We possessed him. We treasured him. Most of our hopes and dreams were confined within him. He was our first-born child! We disciplined him because we wanted to form and mold him to be a man full of wisdom, maturity, and respect. We educated him because we wanted the very best life had to offer him. As the end of high school was within our sights, we dreamed of college and technical training to prepare him for a solid career. And we dreamed of the kind of wife for him who would joyfully desire to be our daughter. A daughter would complete our family, raise our grandchildren, all while making our son happy. We hoped for not only grandchildren but eventually great-grandchildren to carry on the family name. And all in an instant, all our hopes and dreams for him came to a tragic end.

If I made a list of all the things which are tough about grief the list of items would surely be in the hundreds by now. I am certain the list would continue to grow with time. After the loss, the grief just goes on and on. I have no choice but to accept there is no end and no boundary for grief here on this earth. However, we have come to realize heaven will be the end of our grief. We have identified God's Word, prayer, and the body of Christ (the church) as keys to the healing process. Sure, there will always be something new which creeps up and causes the wound to be reopened, just like a big extra-strength adhesive bandage ripped from the skin and a dose of salt poured into the wound causing sting and echoes of pain deep into the heart. But I have a High Priest who I can turn to when those events happen. [10]

One of the most frustrating and hurtful things for the grieving community is the people you encounter who cannot sympathize. I cannot expect everyone to sympathize. After all, they haven't gone through it and therefore cannot begin to grasp the subject matter. I must remember before 2009, I myself was unaware of the impact of a very personal close loss. I tried to understand. I tried to relate but I could not fully understand the pain created by permanent absence. Shockingly, I am overwhelmed by the number of people I meet who have no real concern for the hurting. Some of the most unlikely people and in some of the most unlikely of places would be a source of deep pain and depression for me personally, causing further alienation. It is a frequent struggle for me to fight to overcome the desire to be alone and in the comfort and security of my home. If it were up to me, I would find it easy to become a hermit and live inside the confines of my home. However, there is a calling. And, it's a constant calling. In depression I know my soul always finds the instruction it needs inside God's Word. I often find my reading of His Word to land me in places in the Bible where I am reminded to leave my water pot and tell the others[11] or to teach the younger women[12] or reminded I am an ambassador for Christ[13] or to confess Him before men[14] or teach[15] or sing of My praises[16] or go tell the others[17]. I am often prompted that He has entrusted me[18] with His testimony. I gasp upon reading and being reminded over and over in scripture the word "*entrusted*". It's always my command from Him to keep persevering and moving forward to fulfill my purpose for what He has called me to finish. He certainly knows how to keep me moving in His direction and not my own. If it were up to my carnal flesh, I would protect myself from the world. But we can protect ourselves right out of our holy work for God. The enemy (Satan) would love to bundle you up for your own comfort to keep you away from the darkness of the world. He loves to intimidate those with a testimony because they are a threat to the devil's domain. I must rely on the spiritual and not the carnal for my direction. And, I must gather my direction from God's Most Holy Word--His Bible.

The lack of understanding for the grieving has helped me to see the agony Jesus went through to die for the sins of all mankind. He would die a torturous death while knowing most (the majority) would never accept His gift of grace. Because His pain was much greater than mine could ever be, I can look to Him as my High Priest! He bore the ultimate sacrifice—His perfect sinless life! I am nothing compared to my precious Savior!

Hebrews 2:17 (NKJV) *Therefore, in all things He had to be made like His brethren, that He might be a merciful and faithful High Priest in things pertaining to God, to make propitiation for the sins of the people. For in that He Himself has suffered, being tempted, He is able to aid those who are tempted.*

Be sure and read that again, "In all things He had to be made like His brethren." Why? So, He would be merciful and so He could give aid to those who are suffering.

God continually reminds us we cannot find comfort in anyone or anything but Him. We will never obtain healing through man for our grief. For the people of the Old Testament, they went through a priest for the atonement of their sins. But when Jesus came to earth, when the "…*Word was made flesh…*" (John 1:14 KJV) He came to know pain. He came to know temptations. He knew pain and sorrow like none other. He was mocked, beaten, persecuted, schemed against, plotted against, attacked and scorned. His own people told lies about Him. The people He helped came to deny Him. The people He fed and loved came to be His betrayer. He died the most horrific crucifixion documented in all of history. It is the most documented death of all time! Jesus knew suffering. Jesus knew the sting of death. He knew death. He knows the inside of the grave!

And, He knows how to sympathize.

Hebrews 2:17 states "*He is able to give aid*". He had to die this unimaginable death to be able to sympathize with mankind. He had to become flesh to become the perfect sacrifice. He abolished the priesthood of the Old Covenant and He became a High Priest who could sympathize with the one falling at His feet for the forgiveness of their sins. The Old Testament priests could fail as they were human. They could even die. But, when Jesus became our High Priest He lives forever, and He never changes.

"But now Jesus, our High Priest, has been given a ministry that is far superior to the old priesthood, for he is the one who mediates for us a far better covenant with God, based on better promises." (Hebrews 7:22 NLT)

There is no one who can say, "Jesus just doesn't understand". There is no one who knows our pain like Jesus. God sent Him as the Son of Man so He would know and understand. There is no greater High Priest!

"For we have not a high priest which cannot be touched with the feeling of our infirmities; but was in all points tempted like as we are, yet without sin." Hebrews 4:15 (KJV)

We cannot expect any kind of empathizing from man to meet up to the High Priest of the Heavenly realm. You will not find it. You can look but you will never find the comfort you need in any other person, even a deep endearing friendship. You will be let down by man over and over as God teaches, trains, molds, and shapes you to understand He is the peace. He is the only one who can understand your pain.

"But we see Jesus, who was made a little lower than the angels for the suffering of death, crowned with glory and honor; that He by the grace of God should taste death for every man." Hebrews 2:9 (NKJV)

For the one who has suffered loss or extreme hardships, you have been entrusted with that loss so you may come to the aid of those who are going through the same type of loss. You can give help and comfort and prayers like none other for those who have been put in your path to help with their grief. This entrustment prepares you for the work He is calling you to perform. God uses people to comfort, but He is the greatest Comforter of them all!

Blessed be God, even the Father of our Lord Jesus Christ, the Father of mercies, and the God of all comfort; Who comforteth us in all our tribulation, that we may be able to comfort them which are in any trouble, by the comfort wherewith we ourselves are comforted of God. (2 Corinthians 1:3-4 KJV)

<u>Rocky Point Principle:</u>

If it were not for the spiritual droughts in our walk,

we would not appreciate the spiritual rains.

Walking Forward When Bad Happens

Over the years since losing Jake, I compiled a list of items I learned in the tough trenches of my spiritual journey. These items have helped me. And, I often share them with others in their dark times. (Please be aware these are in no particular order.)

1. <u>What you do not surrender to God will remain broken.</u> He will not fix what you refuse to surrender. He wants to be your God. He desires your trust and faith to be in Him.

2. <u>If you only focus on what is missing, then you will miss out on life.</u> You will miss out on the living. It may be difficult but count your blessings. I have watched so many who are deep in grief abandon their families mentally because they could not overcome the grave. (I will discuss in greater depth later.)

3. <u>When bad happens, your own strength is weakened.</u> You will need the right kind of strength. Man-made items may provide temporary strength, but they are sure to run dry or become yesterday's fix. Remember, when you are weak, He is strong. It is God who will carry you through the bad, but He wants to walk with you daily in the good and bad times. You will soon learn when the bad comes to visit your life trying to manage it and walk forward will bring not only mental exhaustion but physical exhaustion. Remember this Bible verse: *"He brought me up also out of a horrible pit, out of the miry clay, and set my feet upon a rock, and established my goings."* Psalm 40:2 (KJV) Have you ever tried to walk in miry clay? I know when you take even small steps in miry clay the vacuum pulls you back into the wet and moist engulfing clay. It's hard to walk in the mud and the muck. But what Jesus wants to do is to set your feet upon a solid foundation to make your steps easier. He pulls us out of the miry clay, and He sets our feet upon a solid surface, so our steps are not hard and small, but so our steps can be taken with Him at our side. The miry clay pulls you back in. It is heavy, and it is weighted down with struggle. His firm foundation as Jesus as the rock is liberating, freeing, and allows our feet to move forward rather than be pulled back into the "miry clay".

4. <u>When bad happens, you make a choice—to walk through it with
    God or to walk through it alone.</u> I have watched so many make a
    choice to go through it without Him. I continue to see those who
    don't choose Him to suffer and turn to the wrong tools to get
    through each day. I have seen so many choose alcohol, drugs
    (prescription and illegal substances), toxic relationships, career
    ladders, material items, or even sink more time into their jobs
    while the family decays and breaks apart leading to separation or
    divorce, and ultimately a broken family. The vacuum following
    the loss is a painful one. Choose your remedies wisely. Losses put
    real tension and strain on a family. With Christ at the center, He is
    ready to carry the burden lightening the load.

5. <u>The platform is now yours in a time of tragedy, catastrophe,
    disaster, or loss.</u> God has positioned you in a unique place to now
    share about the God who delivers, transforms, restores, comforts,
    heals, gives good gifts, and who equips the called. It is not one I
    would choose on my own, but I have come to accept He is
    sovereign. I have witnessed glimpses of why He allowed this in
    my life. And from scriptural knowledge, I am reminded I am to be
    the "ambassador for Christ" in no matter the season. (2
    Corinthians 5:20 NKJV)

6. <u>Choose to operate in a mode of encouragement rather than
    discouragement.</u> This is a choice. Discouragement happens when
    we are focused on self. It is quite easy to slip into discouragement.
    The act of encouragement is pouring courage into others. Jesus
    never allowed discouragement to halt His ministry. He was the
    most persecuted person of all time. However, He received His
    encouragement from the Father. Learning to operate in a mode
    where we receive our encouragement from God is of the utmost
    importance while walking through tough times. When we are
    receiving our courage from God, then we can pour courage into
    others going through their storms of life. We receive our courage
    from God through reading His Bible, through prayer, and through
    His unexpected blessings.

7. <u>"Fight" off self-pity.</u> Some days this is a real fight! This is a place
    where the enemy would love for us to remain (not only in times of

grief, but in all situations, hardships, trials, and tests). Sometimes we will look up and take note we have slid into this dangerous area. If we find ourselves in the land of pity, we must remember Matthew 11:28-30 (NKJV): *"Come to Me, all you who labor and are heavy laden, and I will give you rest. Take My yoke upon you and learn from Me, for I am gentle and lowly in heart, and you will find rest for your souls. For My yoke is easy and My burden is light."* Self-pity is a weight. Self-pity (feeling sorry for our circumstances) is not a place where Jesus desires anyone to remain. As I have grown in the Lord, I have discovered the enemy is the one pushing the self-pity agenda. So, if the enemy is the author of self-pity then we should view self-pity as a temptation. (Trust me! It takes a little while to arrive at this learning!) As we walk in the healing power of Jesus, we only glance at our circumstances long enough to know what Jesus has brought us out of, but it is no longer a place where we choose to dwell. We simply cannot grow always looking back. Looking back leads to destructive life patterns, repetitive cycles of failure, and hinders and cripples our spiritual growth. We can only grow spiritually when we reach for the hand of Jesus Christ each day. The walk of a Christ-follower requires one step at a time. The beautiful part of the grace of Jesus Christ is when we stumble, He is always there to shower us with even more love. His grace is a spring which never runs dry.

8. <u>We are all in a battle.</u> During the search and recovery mission of 45 days on Kentucky Lake, there was a home on the same road leading to Rocky Point Bay which burned during the night. A mother and all her children died in that fire. Davy remarked, "There is always someone who has it worse than you. And we have much to be thankful!" And, he was correct. People are in a battle!

9. <u>Ask God for help in trusting Him.</u> For 39 years I had a distrust of God and His ways. I didn't vocalize my suspicion. However, my inner conflict displayed it. In February 2009, I surrendered and put my faith in Him rather than man or things. Sure, I find myself on occasions where I wonder what He is doing, but I must call upon

His grace to help me through those times. Proverbs 3:5 (NKJV) *"Trust in the Lord with all your heart, and lean not on your own understanding."* When bad things happen, I have an opportunity to learn more about trusting Him. I made a conscious effort to accept His ways are higher. Isaiah 55:8 (NKJV) *"'For my thoughts are not your thoughts, nor are your ways My ways,' says the Lord."* Little by little and day by day we learn indeed His ways are much higher than ours.

10. <u>Come to accept He is a "one step at a time" God</u>. He is a good teacher. A good teacher teaches slowly and repeats so you can learn depth versus superficially. He doesn't move at the speed we desire Him to move, but when He moves, He does more in one second than a person can do in a lifetime.

11. <u>Learn to appreciate death teaches us more about life than life could ever teach us about life.</u> What does this mean? Death causes us to stop and to pause and to review life. When we are deep into life, busy into daily routine, focused on crossing off the lists and mundane tasks, we find it difficult to consciously make daily decisions which add depth to life. But, when we are faced with the death of a close loved one, there is a long pause and suddenly we review the past, fast forward, and back it up just like one would rewind, pause, or fast-forward a movie. We rewind, fast-forward, pause, rewind, replay, revisit, relive, and wish. We wish we had done things differently. We notice after a major crisis, our reasoning and decision-making skills change. Again, death creates in us a different view of life: to savor the aroma of life in simplicity.

12. <u>Fight the "hermit syndrome"</u>. Avoid slipping back into withdrawal when people don't say the right things. Before 2009, I thought I knew what it felt like to suffer loss, but it had not become my reality. Even today people still say things that bother me, but it's different now. I have the Lord to ask for help. One day while studying in the Word of God it was revealed to me: *Luke 6:37 (NKJV) "Judge not, and you shall not be judged. Condemn not, and you shall not be condemned. Forgive, and you will be forgiven.* And again, in Ephesians 4:32 (NKJV) *"And be kind to*

one another, tenderhearted, forgiving one another, even as God in Christ forgave you. " Christ died the ultimate sacrifice for me. When we examine our own shortcomings, we realize we need His forgiveness every day. There was no one more taunted, persecuted, mocked, and abused than Christ. Yet He was perfect. Immediately in my heart, I was overwhelmed with His grace. And because I have received His grace as hard as it may be, I can grant grace to others. I knew I was trying to hold others to a standard which even I could not uphold. Before 2009, I was blind to the loss of a child. I knew what it was like to lose someone close, but I didn't know what it was like to lose my beloved child. I did not know what it was like to lose a child I had carried in my womb, watched grow and develop, held and nurtured, dreamed of futures abounding, and who was the light and joy of all my days. Now, when people try to speak of things they do not understand, I remember and mumble those verses in my quiet spirit and walk on and become thankful they do not know what it is like to lose a child. Yes, I am thankful they do not know the pain. God is always willing to teach us and walk us step by step through grief if we allow Him the opportunity.

13. <u>Accept people fail.</u> We all fail. We all fail miserably. So, resist the temptation to judge when others fail. When people fail to call out their name and even fail you at birthdays and anniversaries forgive and then move on. Remember, people have a hard time remembering the birthdays and anniversaries of the living. People in your close circle do not forget your loved one. But they do forget important dates. Know this with all certainty: people will fail you, but God will never fail you. We are human. God is perfect. His love never fails. His love never runs dry. His comfort is never empty. He has no boundaries. He is enough for me! Coming to the place in tough times to say, "God is enough for me!" is critical. It's in that place we are surrendered to Him in fullness. And what we surrender to Him He will surely give back to us more than we could have ever imagined, dreamed, or anticipated. Trust Him!

14. Examine the throne of the heart. In Exodus 20:1-3 (NKJV) *And God spoke all these words, saying: "I am the Lord your God, who brought you out of the land of Egypt, out of the house of bondage. "You shall have no other gods before Me."* There came a day when I realized I had put my son, Jake, on the throne of my heart and he had become one of my many gods. Please do not misunderstand. We are supposed to love our family. But I had placed him above the priority of a relationship with my Father. I had to turn loose and put God on the throne of my heart. Once I did, I discovered how God began to heal and comfort. I began to see Him move and work in a whole new way. My advice: "let go and let God" --anonymous. It does not mean I don't love Jake. It doesn't mean I am not sad for all the hopes and dreams I had for Jake. What it means is that God is now in a place in my life of priority above Jake, above my husband, above my son, Hunter, above my home, above my work and material goods. He gives us a spiritual filling each day to be all we need to be for our family when we place Him as priority. God brought me out of the house of bondage of grief-stricken sadness without hope.

15. For the believer of Jesus Christ, we have a Helper. John 14:16 (NKJV) *"And I will pray the Father, and He shall give you another Comforter, that He may abide with you forever."* Because of His love for a relationship with us He sent a Comforter (the Holy Spirit) to live inside us to help us with our grief, our loss, our trials, or our hurts. He lives in the heart of the believer. This great Comforter will flood your heart and soul with peace. (I will discuss in greater depth in the next chapter.)

16. Accept Jesus' blood as the payment for your sins. It's free. All you must do is ask. If you have not come to a place and time where you have placed your faith, trust, and confidence in the blood of Jesus Christ for the removal of your sins, my prayer is for you to do so. I pray you will remember this forever and ever. Do not think for one moment you can clean yourself up enough to come to Him without blemish. But, just go to Him exactly as you are and where you are. The first step is salvation (being rescued by God through Jesus Christ), then sanctification (the cleaning up

process). The biggest hindrance to coming to Jesus (other than disbelief and doubt) is getting sanctification in the wrong order. For 39 years I believed I was not clean enough to come to Him and so I failed Him miserably. I would try to clean up my act, then attend church, only to find myself failing again as soon as church let out. But what we must do is exactly as Jesus says, "come".[19] I encourage you to pray to the Father and ask Him to forgive you of all your sins, then tell Him you believe His Son, Jesus was sent to this world to die for your sins, that He died on the Cross, and that He arose from the dead 3 days later, and He ascended to the Father and sits at His right hand. Ask Him for His Son, Jesus, to come and make you whole and complete. Desire to make Jesus the Lord of your ways and desires. If you do this then He sends the Comforter to come and take up residence in you. Now, my friend, you will find healing and comfort that no other can provide. Dive into God's Holy Word, the Holy Bible, each day. Pray and carry on a daily conversation with the Father because you have been made righteous before the Father through Jesus' Christ perfect blood. Now you can *come boldly before the throne of grace* (Hebrews 4:16 KJV) in prayer anywhere and anytime. The Holy Spirit will then begin cleaning you up for good work. Remember, don't reverse the order. It is salvation first, then sanctification. Not, sanctification, then salvation. This is a hindrance to the majority. They see the cleanup required to come to Jesus Christ. The enemy loves to keep sanctification and salvation backwards so he can maintain authority and rule over his people. Jesus says, *"Come to Me…"* (Matthew 11:28 NAS) Jesus desires us to come to Him then He will grant us the power to overcome the costs we see with our eyes.

17. The right church is crucial. The church should be where the Word of God is taught and learned. Unfortunately, not all of today's churches adhere to the Bible. Find a church which teaches the whole authoritative Word of God and begin connecting with others. Beware of cults and man-made religion. Beware of religion that teaches from an adulterated manual. The Word of God is the Truth. It is the book which distinguishes the real church

from a social club. The Word of God magnifies truth and extinguishes religion. When people remove or manipulate verses from His Bible, they remove power from their own lives and from the church. They render themselves powerless in His work. Jesus looks for relationship and not religion. Jesus hates and despises religion. Review His many conversations with the Pharisees and Chief Priests in the Gospel. Lastly, you will find help and healing through good members of the Body of Christ (the church) who have been through similar circumstances. These relationships are encouraging and supportive in your walk.

18. <u>Prayer is your lifeline.</u> One cannot learn someone unless they study them. Studying a person comes by talking to them, listening to them, asking them questions, and awaiting a response. One can never learn God without this intimate conversation. This is where you learn God's nature and ways. Prayer will become your lifeline. But you must pray in order to experience God at work in your life. Pray, believe, and keep your eyes open.

19. <u>With every feeling of negative emotion immediately enter into conversation with God.</u> These negative times are a call to prayer and communion with Him. These are triggers to pray! It is neat how He designed us to have a signal (our emotions) to pray.

20. <u>Daily ask God to show you ways you are grieving the Holy Spirit.</u> When the Holy Spirit is given liberty to work in our lives we are growing. During these times we see and experience the work of God in our lives. (I will discuss further in the upcoming chapter).

21. <u>Help others.</u> We are not here on this earth for ourselves and our own selfish desires despite the world's teachings. We were created to serve and worship a Holy God. God put us here with a purpose. Part of serving Him is to serve His people. We are the church outside the walls of the church operating for the good of the kingdom. I will give you an example: January 10, 2017, was the 8-year anniversary of the duck hunting accident. This was a sad and dreary day. I remember the cold drizzle of the day and I was sad all morning. The memories always flood your mind with thoughts of where you were at each passing hour of the day. My phone rang that morning and it was my friend, Amanda. Her mom

and dad's house was on fire. This was the second home they had lost to fire! Amanda was crying and upset. Davy and I put on our rain jackets and headed out the door to be with the family. The fire was extinguished. As we could enter, we went in and packed out items from the attached grandmother's apartment hauling them to a nearby storage unit. Afterwards, our Pastor Keith and friends gathered in a nearby restaurant. When the group of us volunteers walked into the restaurant, sat down at the table, ordered our food, the song came over the intercom speakers: *Feed Jake*[20]. Then we looked at one another and smiled. My pastor who knew our story remarked, "I don't know whether to smile or to cry. I just don't know." So, as Pastor Ronnie taught us early in grief: "When you are down, go and help someone." He was right once again. We received a blessing from helping those in need that day. And I must believe God rewarded with some comfort and at the perfect time! God blesses us when we bless others in need. I have seen this time and time again in my own experiences. (I no longer listen to country music. I focus on feeding my mind with good encouraging things. Country music is something I found it to be very depressing to my spirit. I found it to put my mind in a very bad place. I replaced it with Christian worship music which is sure to lift and encourage the spirit.)

22. Every day we are composing our own obituary. Every day we are writing our own final sermon to be preached at our funeral. I don't want mine to say that I loved to embark on an internet streaming binge-watching television obsession, or I wasted time on social media, or that I played useless games on my smartphone, or that I embarked in other time-draining hobbies and travels. Instead, I would rather it say that my life was changed forever because of Jesus Christ, and my life set out to glorify my Maker, my Creator, the Lover of my soul, Jesus Christ. Let that be the only glory in my death! His name be glorified! I have much love to return to Him not only because of the Comfort He has provided me but because of His abundant supply of grace!

23. Life is a sermon. Each day our life is preaching a sermon to those around us. I have attended funerals of those who I did not know

personally. I knew their loved one, but I really did not know them. I attended out of respect for their loved one left behind. However, I learned much about them during their funeral. I have found that sometimes the preacher preaches the funeral and sometimes the person lying in the casket is doing the preaching. Yes, some preached their whole life in the way they lived, and their life would continue to preach the sermon even though they had left this walk of life. Now, that is a legend! And this is a legacy we should all long to leave behind. A legacy is one where even though we have left this earth, our life continues to reach, teach, or preach the kingdom of God.

24. I highly recommend journaling. A notebook is a safe place to house your feelings. I could feel a tug on my heart to write this book very early in this process. However, I did not fully realize what else God had in store as we began to slowly write each chapter. It was confirmed when we had many people come to us and tell us we needed to write a book. I cannot possibly tell you in words how difficult it was to be forced to recall dark times in our life and put them on paper. However, there was a huge blessing as we neared the end of the book's completion. We began to proofread, recalled the diary of events, and remembered how God had moved and worked in certain situations. It was a blessing to see our son, Hunter, be able to share in the history and events. He will have this book with him forever to help him navigate life.

25. His grace can carry you through any circumstance. Stay plugged into Him. Imagine yourself as a plug-in needing power and He is the only power source. When you unplug yourself from Him, you lose power (strength).

The Grave

The past several years I have had the honor of speaking with others who are going through the storms of life suffering financial loss, divorces, or other extreme hardships. I also cross paths with those grieving the loss of their beloved. Many seek a quick fix to heal their grief. By nature, we long to return to normal—the ways things used to be! And, we want to find peace fast. We long for what is missing from our life. The thing, person, or relationship which satisfied us and brought us great joy is missing. This sadness and heaviness will overpower us if we allow it.

I have been asked repeatedly, "Ok, so how can I learn to live again?" There is a key to grief and please be patient with me as I take you down this path. It will be well worth your patience. I promise! If you actively engage in these things you will find the greatest peace you have ever known. Maybe you have already found peace. This will still be worth your time. This will help you to grow in peace and comfort no matter your circumstances.

First, we need to understand grief. Grief is an emotion which contains other emotions. Within grief there is anger, guilt, shame, fear, doubt, sadness, hopelessness, alienation, and even brief moments of joy. At the peak of grief, the brief moments of joy come when we recall precious memories of our loved one. The emotion of grief is felt when we lose relationship with a loved one. "The word *grief* comes from the Latin word *gravare*, which means to make heavy. *Gravare* itself comes from the Latin word *gravis*, which means weighty. So, think of grief as a heavy, oppressive sadness. We associate it most often with mourning a loved one's death, but it can follow any kind of loss."[21] And, of course, we know the meaning of the noun *grave*. A grave is the location we place the deceased. The word grave also originates from the Latin word *gravis*.[22]

Before we can find our source of healing for grief we must return to the grave for learning.

Are you overcoming the grave?

or

Is the grave overcoming you?

Grief comes from the grave. Before we can be healed from grief, we must rely on the One who was in the grave for three days and lived to tell about it. Jesus Christ overcame the grave! By drawing from His strength, we can overpower the weight of the grave. Any emotional stronghold can be conquered when we place our faith in the overcomer.

Jesus came to die to pay an overwhelming penalty. When we examine our lives against The Ten Commandments, we realize we are sinful people. There is none of us worthy to stand in the presence of God the Father and say we have been good. We have all broken laws. In fact, I have broken laws which I did not know were laws. None of us are good. We may remark, "he or she is a good person." However, our comparison for goodness and purity is against the standard which is God. God is pure and holy and cannot look upon sin. In Leviticus 19:2 KJV *"Speak unto all the congregation of the children of Israel, and say unto them, Ye shall be holy: for I the Lord your God am holy."* God commands holiness. The problem is this: we cannot be holy for only a few minutes at a time until a bad thought comes into our mind or a desire for something unholy consumes us. So, how can we be holy? Only through faith in Jesus Christ can we be made holy. *"For He hath made Him to be sin for us, who knew no sin; that we might be made the righteousness of God in Him."* (2 Corinthians 5:21 KJV) So, the only way we can be made righteous before God and to stand in the very presence of God is by being made righteous. And the only way to be made righteous is to believe in Jesus Christ, the Savior. *"If you openly declare that Jesus is Lord and believe in your heart that God raised Him from the dead, you will be saved."* (Romans 10:9 NLT)

To return to the grave for healing, let's return to what we know about Jesus Christ. He came to live a sinless life. He was crucified for us to pay the ransom for our sins. Jesus faced hell so we wouldn't have to face hell. He paid the death sentence in our place. In today's language, Jesus came to bail us out of prison for which we were on death row. We were sentenced to die and to die a horrible death being banished from the presence of God Almighty Father of the heavens because we have nothing good inside of us to save us. Jesus Christ came and bailed us out! He paid our jail fees! He saved us from death row! And, we just like Barabbas at the cross of Calvary were set free because of Jesus, the perfect sacrifice for our sins. Barabbas and Jesus stood before the governor and the people were asked which one should die. The chief priests taunted the crowds into making Jesus the one to go to the Cross of Calvary. The leaders were jealous of the attention Jesus received from the mass crowds. They wanted Him gone! Just as the Old Testament prophesied, only a spotless, blemish-free lamb could be sacrificed for the atonement of sins. And, so God had control of all circumstances all along. Even in the most horrible and horrific event of all of history, God was in control. Barabbas was freed even though he deserved to die for his crimes. (Barabbas was the one who should have died because he was a murderer and Jesus was sinless). However, Jesus willingly walked to the Cross of Calvary. [23] He died for the sins of all mankind. He was placed in a tomb (a grave). And just as Jesus promised to His Disciples, He overcame the grave. He was raised to life on the third day. He appeared first to Mary Magdalene at the empty tomb.[24] He went to His Disciples to speak to them. He went to "doubting Thomas" to show him His scars.[25] Thomas believed in Him with such passion and such vigor that he too would travel as far as India to preach the Gospel Good News of Jesus Christ.[26] The "doubting Thomas" made such a huge impact in India converting many people to become Jesus followers. Due to religious persecution, Thomas was speared to death in India. But, Thomas' testimony and his sharing of the Good News of the Gospel of Christ had such dynamic bearing on people. Some of his converts traveled to a deserted island and named the island, St. Thomas, establishing a church named after the former "doubting Thomas"![27] Isn't it amazing how the things we see today point back today to Jesus Christ?

Jesus had this influence on all His Disciples except for one, Judas, the famous traitor. Jesus' ministry through His life, His death, His burial, His resurrection, His ascension on the Mount of Olives had such a tremendous influence on changing the hearts and lives of people. These Disciples were willing to suffer great torture, persecution, and ultimately death to preach the Good News. Their belief and the power of the Holy Spirit gave them the power to overcome their fears.

Before we can fully grasp the Good News of Jesus Christ we must understand first, the bad news. The bad news as I formerly mentioned is no one is holy and righteous of themselves. We are bad people. We are evil people. We have nothing within us which can stand before the Holy God of this universe. Only because of faith in Jesus Christ for the payment of our sins can we be made holy.

If you have accepted Jesus Christ, then you have the power to overcome the grave. You will never taste death, but as Psalms 23:4 (NKJV) explains "the shadow of death". As a born-again believer in Jesus Christ, we will only know "the shadow of death". *"We are confident, I say, and prefer rather to be absent from the body and to be at home with the Lord."* (2 Corinthians 5:8 NAS) Jesus offers eternal life. And because of Him, the end is not the end. The grave is not final.

You can overcome grief because of Jesus' victory over the grave. We can overcome because of Jesus Christ. By placing our focus on the only One who overcame the grave we can find healing from grief. The heaviness and the burdening we feel during grief can be eased by relying on Jesus Christ to take that grief, placing our faith in Him to heal us. *"Blessed are those who mourn, for they shall be comforted."* (Matthew 5:4 KJV)

Many people have made professions of faith, but they have missed something of tremendous importance, the work of the Holy Spirit. Jesus said in John chapter 14:15-18 (NKJV), *"If you love Me, keep My commandments. And I will pray the Father, and He will give you another Helper that He may abide with you forever—"the Spirit of truth, whom the world cannot receive, because it neither sees Him nor knows Him; but you know Him, for He dwells with you and will be in you. "I will not leave you orphans I will come to you."*

Jesus taught His Disciples about the capital "H" Helper in John 14:16. The King James translation refers to Him as "Comforter". CSB translation refers to Him as a "Counselor". NLT refers to Him as "Advocate". The person of the Holy Spirit is all those things: Comforter, Counselor, Advocate.

But, what did Jesus say before He spoke about the Holy Spirit of Promise? In John 14:15 (NKJV), "If you love Me, keep My commandments." Jesus asked us to obey His commandments. Then, in verse 16 He explains about the Helper He will send. You cannot serve who you do not love. It is work! We show our love by obeying Him. Disobedience is the act of rebellion which will quench or grieve the work of the Holy Spirit in our lives. Notice verse 15 is conditional "If". It depends on obedience, love, and the act which stems from love. This Comforter, the Holy Spirit is a powerful force. He indeed comforts, advocates for us, and counsels us. And, we require the Holy Spirit to help us overcome.

The Apostle Paul speaks in-depth about the Holy Spirit. In Ephesians chapter 4 Paul writes about the new man in verses 17 through 22. In verse 23-24 (NKJV) he writes, "*and be renewed in the spirit of your mind, and that you put on the new man which was created according to God, in true righteousness and holiness.*" First, we must "*put on the new man*". We do that by accepting Jesus Christ's gift of grace. Paul then writes about ways we may grieve the Holy Spirit's work in our lives. In verses 25 – 32 Paul lists the specific ways we may grieve the Holy Spirit. In verse 30 He states, "*And do not grieve the Holy Spirit of God by whom you were sealed for the day of redemption.*" He continues in Ephesians chapter 5 verse 1 to encourage us to "be imitators of God as dear children". I challenge you to read the entire book of Ephesians. It will certainly help you in growing as a Christ-follower. With application of these verses, it will help you to live as a victorious Christian rather than a defeated Christian.

We grieve the Holy Spirit of God by acting in disobedience. When that happens, our spiritual growth is stopped. Though we were sealed for the day of redemption we can stunt our own growth spiritually. And, let me tell you personally, it is painful. The Holy Spirit will not make the work of disobedience comfortable for you. His job is to prepare the bride to meet the bridegroom. The bridegroom is Jesus. The Holy Spirit's job is to make us beautiful to meet Him. He comes and begins cleaning out, convicting, and changing our heart's desires. He convicts of sin and encourages us to deal with repentance and turning from the sin. No relationship can be reconciled (made right) without true repentance.

Yes, we are a long way from holy, but day by day by surrendering ourselves to the grave we are lifted out being made new each day (if we will submit and come under the authority of God). God blesses a heart of genuine repentance. I have witnessed this time and time again! We must be prepared to investigate our lives for where sin is hiding and stand ready to remove it. God blesses sin removal! He showers the abundance of His love each time we come to Him apologizing for our sins.

By God's divine nature He keeps us close to Him by the work of His Holy Spirit indwelling. I have always found the wisdom of God to be mind-blowing. Only a Triune God could do something so amazing.

When we grieve the Holy Spirit, He is grieved because of a loss of fellowship or relationship with us. We grieve when we lose a loved one. We ache and agonize for the fellowship we once had with our loved one. The Holy Spirit grieves for us to restore our relationship with Him. He grieves because He has lost fellowship with us. Think about the pain for just a moment and meditate on that. He is asking us to walk this road to make us ready to meet Christ. And, we are walking in rebellion. He is grieved because of our disobedience. I hope this puts things in the right perspective for you as you seek to grow spiritually in the Lord.

In my own personal life, I encountered a time of deep depression and darkness. I did not know or understand what was occurring. I was much too ashamed to speak about what was happening. There were only a few who I believe might understand the depth of the depression. And, so I was forced to go to work, engage in the daily tasks, and fight through it as best as I could. I could not drop my pride and ask anyone to pray for me for fear of being judged.

What helped restore me and bring me out of the darkness of the depression was the realization I was grieving the Holy Spirit in my grief walk. God was wanting me to place Him first in my life. I have found a pattern. When I am not engaging in certain activities there is a loss of joy and I sink into depression. The spiritual depression comes when I have damaged my relationship with Him. I have grieved Him. And, I recognized through repetition of failures I was starving myself from His fellowship by my own free will. Over the past years, I have learned to recognize when the relationship alarms are sounding. I have learned in my selfishness my spiritual depression thrives and flourishes. And, when I begin serving, praising, and being submissive to God my joy returns. Yes, I have learned how to restore intimacy and not to starve Him out of fellowship. We ring heaven's doorbell when we: 1.) Praise Him. 2.) Obey

Him and serve Him out of love. 3.) Submit to His Word. 4.) Operate with a heart of repentance and sorrow for our sin. 5.) Remain in a mode of conversation with Him throughout our day. (Please note, this is not an exhaustive list, but I have learned to look in one of these areas when my spiritual alarms are sounding.) Now, notice I didn't use the word prayer in #5? In today's world people have lost the true meaning of prayer. Prayer is conversing with God and then listening. Communication is made up of speaking and listening. After the conversation listen to God. He speaks. He speaks through His Word. He speaks through events or circumstances. He speaks through people. He speaks through His creations. He speaks through His Holy Spirit. He speaks through that "still small voice" (1 Kings 19:12 KJV). (This list is also not exhaustive.) He repeats verses for us so we can be taught by Him. He brings peace during times of decisions. Or, He brings anxiety to keep us from making wrong decisions. He gently guides us as the good and gentle Shepherd guides His sheep to greener pastures.

Let's examine the Holy Spirit from another angle. If you are inviting a very special dinner guest to your home for dinner you would set the table for them. You might find a special tablecloth, fine linen napkins, perfectly placed silverware, matching plates, bowls, and cups. You might even light some candles on the table to establish an inviting climate. Because they are a special guest and because you cherish their fellowship you want to do what it takes to make the environment appealing for them. Why? You want them to know they are special, and you spent extra care preparing for their visit. It is a show of affection and hospitality for your special guest.

Now, relate this principle to the Holy Spirit. The Holy Spirit is the flowing living Spirit from a Holy Triune God who came to live and dwell in your tabernacle (your heart) once you accepted the salvation of Jesus Christ. He dwells in the heart, but He can become grieved and He can become quenched. His welcoming environment is a heart willing to be obedient to His direction, willing to prioritize time for His presence, and one whose heart is prepared to listen. He is thrilled with a heart ready to say "yes" to His direction. Treat Him with all respect and dignity and set up a fostering atmosphere for His stay in your heart. Welcome the Holy

Spirit daily to speak to you. Prepare a place, a time, and set the table of your heart. I promise He will fill your cup every day and He will provide direction through His Holy Word. The Holy Spirit thrives in an environment where the heart believes in every word of His most Holy Bible. Belief does not stop at the name of Jesus, but it believes also in His Bible. There is power in His Word. Remember, Jesus is the Word. (John 1:14) By applying these principles, you will not grieve the Spirit of God, but rather you will invite and nurture His daily re-filling. You will begin to mature spiritually, and you will discover an unending source of healing, comfort, peace, and joy. Yes, when you set the table you will experience the nearness of God! And the feast will be nourishing to your spirit.

Now, isn't it amazing how the God of the universe keeps us close and in communication with Him? I believe it is. He loves us all so very much! He craves fellowship and relationship with His beloved children.

Rocky Point Principles:

No relationship can be reconciled without true repentance.

Every day we make a choice to either grieve

the Holy Spirit or to nurture Him.

The key to healing is the welcoming of the Holy Spirit.

The Holy Spirit is welcomed by a heart ready to say, "Yes!".

God blesses sin removal.

To Hunter with love…

My warm, kind-hearted, blue-eyed, baby boy, my "Mr. Hunter", my "H-man", Hunter,

No matter your age, you will always be my baby. You are still young (16 years of age) as I complete the writing of this testimony of God's work in my life.

Please cherish the fact this book contains your history and legacy. On days when you are low, may you look back at the ways God moved and showed His great glory. May you be lifted immediately within your spirit each time you read this book. He has revealed His marvelous grandeur knitting together special people and events in life's tapestry. To us, He has revealed His great restoration and His unique mind-boggling comfort. He revealed a perfectly composed plan in each of our lives. His thumbprints on my life can be traced back to His loving hands drawing me to Him.

Allow no one to tell you God is dead, God is not real, or His Bible is not relevant for today. Remember, Jesus Christ is only alive in the hearts of the true believer. His work is not seen in the eyes of the unbeliever. The skeptic has never received His salvation. To have salvation we must first accept God's grace through His Son, Jesus Christ's blood as the penalty for our sins. As Jesus went to the Cross at Calvary stripped down to nothing, we must also come to the Cross. We come with nothing of our own asking for God to give us grace. Then, the Holy Spirit comes to dwell in us when we accept this gift. Once we have the Holy Spirit then we can begin to see things in the spiritual realm. In other words, we can begin to see things God's way. God reveals these mysteries only to those who believe. Humbly I tell you this: Your mom was once lost, but now I am found. Your mom was once spiritually blind, but now I can see.

God made you and He created you in all His glory. He desires for you to become Christ-like. As you have already experienced in your young life, the Cross of Christ is heavy and hard to carry. Life is not always easy, but God allows us these struggles to change and mold us. As there are seasons in life we are changed. He molds and makes us with these seasons. Life is not always fair, but God is in control. When we are weak,

He gives us strength. Rely on Him and His power, not your own. Your strength runs out, but His power is never-ending. May you always stay the course with Jesus as the Lord and Savior of your life. If He is indeed Lord of your life, then He will be your decision-maker. And never forget: It is these things which ring God's doorbell: 1.) Praise Him. 2.) Obey Him and serve Him out of love. 3.) Submit to His Word. 4.) Operate with a heart of repentance and sorrow for your sin. 5.) Remain in a mode of conversation with Him throughout your day.

Never forget God is a Holy God. Respect Him and love Him back for all He has blessed us with in our lives--Grace. If all God bestowed upon you is Jesus Christ, then you are a rich powerful grace-filled man! As you grow to understand more and more about the Grace of God through His Son Jesus Christ, you will come to love God more and more. Once you love God you cannot help but serve God and His people. When He guides your life, you will long to tell others about Him and you will want to grow His kingdom. As you grow spiritually you will desire to seek His will and purpose for your life each day. He has a plan for your life. Seek Him and you will find the plan. Don't seek the plan. Seek Him and He will reveal the plan through the power of the Holy Spirit which lives in you. Please don't get that confused or you will find yourself wandering in the wilderness just like the children of Israel.

I pray you never get caught up in the accumulation of wealth, power, or career revisiting the mistakes your parents made once in life. Please don't make those mistakes! None of those things can be taken with you when you leave this life. Those facades will leave you as a slave because they are never fulfilling. There is never enough money. There is always more to be made. There is never enough control or power. There is always more to be obtained. There is always another step up the career ladder. Remember, everyone, no matter how high up the career ladder, has a boss. But, in God, there is life and work balance. If He oversees your decisions, He manages your time, giving a perfect equilibrium to the chaos of life. Remember this: *"Everything you truly need in life can be found on your deathbed. For on your deathbed nothing will matter except your faith, your family, and your friends."* --anonymous

We have learned the hard way about parenting. I have learned good parenting sets the stage, paves the path, so the child comes to know Jesus

Christ, our Lord and Savior, so that one day the child comes to know Jesus in a personal relationship. What better gift could you give your child one day? This is the ultimate accomplishment in this life: to accept Jesus Christ as your Savior.

Hunter, in our old life we went to church only if it worked into our schedule. But Hunter, please don't make our mistakes. Please stay committed to the Lord and to His Church. God honors and blesses commitment and persistence. I long to see you worshipping with your entire family in church one day and being committed to Him because He committed Himself to you first. Please don't forsake the church. Our commitment to the church displays outwardly our commitment to Christ.

"not forsaking our own assembling together, as is the habit of some, but encouraging one another; and all the more as you see the day drawing near." (Hebrews 10:25 NAS)

He will bring you to a career and bless you in ways unimaginable. Hold onto material things loosely and grasp hold of God with all your might. As you already know, everything we see with our eyes can be taken away from us in the storms of life. In just one phone call, in just one bad instinct, in just one second, in just one raging storm, in just one wave coming over the boat, life (as we know it) can change. Yet, our faith in God can never be shaken or taken. He has proven Himself indeed the Anchor in times of the storm.

Follow God and you will never go wrong. Trust God because He always has your back. Never put your faith in man because you will be let down. It's only a matter of time. After all, we are human. We fail. And we fail one another. But rather, always place your faith in God. God is the same forever and ever. He never changes. His love is an unhuman kind of love so never try to confine His compassion with human definition. That would be so unfair to His majesty. He loves like no other. The mind cannot explain it, nor can we grasp the vastness of how He draws us to Him with His endless love.

It's hard for me to imagine how God could love you any more than we do, but yes, indeed, He does. After all, He gave it all for you. He gave Heaven's Best, Heaven's Darling, Heaven's Crowned Glory, Heaven's

Only Way, Jesus Christ, for you. Never take your eyes off the Cross and all it means to our inheritance as a child of God. I pray your heritage, your upbringing become your legacy. I pray your legacy leads thousands and thousands to Christ. I pray you plant seeds of faith no matter where you travel. Scatter seeds everywhere. Do it with boldness and courage because of His great love. Scatter them with love and admiration for our Father in Heaven. And for those who do not receive you remember Jesus' instructions to His Disciples in Matthew 10:14 (KJV): "…shake off the dust of your feet." Then, Hunter, move forward keeping your eyes focused on the prize of Heaven. You will have people who will reject you, but don't let it control your momentum for Christ's kingdom. Stay the course, my son!

Your big brother would be so very proud of you. Your parents "ooze with joy" at the very sight of you.

Love,
Mom & Dad

Special Thanks To The Following:

Our faithful friends, our faithful prayer warriors, all first responders, Kentucky and Illinois Departments of Natural Resources, Kentucky Game & Wildlife, Team Watters, Herb and Carroll Co. volunteers, Gary, Red Cross Disaster Relief, all emergency workers, all rescue and recovery workers, area dive teams, Robin & the late Rosco, the late Beth Inman, area canine units and leaders, horseback teams, helicopter teams, all volunteers, all area churches, all area pastors, Bro. Ronnie Stinson, Sr. & Pam, Bro. Keith Allred & Cindy, Pastor Mike Donald, Bro. Ronnie Stinson, Jr. & Melanie, the families of Trevor Williams, the families of Mckenzie Stanley, Tyler Heathcott and family, the late Sheriff Dewayne Redmond, Marshall County, Graves County, Marshall County Coroner's office, McCracken County, Byrn Funeral Home, our church families of Chief Cornerstone Baptist Church, Trace Creek Baptist Church, and First Assembly of God, Morningstar Foods Company, Lubrizol Corporation, Royal Crown Bottling Company, all co-workers, area businesses, state and local government, area county law enforcement agencies, National Weather Service, West Kentucky Rural Electric Cooperative, Mayfield High School, Graves County High School, Sabrina Morris, our families, our siblings: Marcia, Anthony, Patrick, Sheri, Angie, Bobby, Mary, Chrissy; our parents, Bob and Mary; and last but not least, Hunter for giving us overwhelming happiness.

References

[1] Sir Edward Elgar, *Pomp & Circumstance Marches*, 1901

[2] Sonny Dean, *Feed Jake*, Pirates of the Mississippi, 1991, Capitol Records Nashville

[3] *Twister*, https://en.wikipedia.org/wiki/Twister_(1996_film), referenced May, 2016

[4] Sonny Dean, *Feed Jake*, Pirates of the Mississippi, 1991, Capitol Records Nashville

[5] Kentucky Lake, https://en.wikipedia.org/wiki/Kentucky_Lake, referenced April 6, 2017

[6] *Courier Newspaper* (February 9, 2009 article), Savannah, Tennessee, accessed March 2009 online via https://www.google.com

[7] *The Holy Spirit: His Seed*, Prime Time with God Devotional, 2004, excerpt from 365 Ways to Know God, Elmer L. Towns, accessed July 23, 2019

[8] Statistics about the Bible, http://www.biblestudy101.org/Lists/statisticsHB.html, accessed July 19, 2019

[9] *Twister*, https://en.wikipedia.org/wiki/Twister_(1996_film)

[10] Hebrews 4:15 KJV

[11] John 4:1-42

[12] Titus 2:3-5

[13] 2 Corinthians 5:20 KJV

[14] Luke 12:8 KJV

[15] Deuteronomy 11:19

[16] Psalm 104:33, Psalm 105:2

[17] Matthew 28:5-8

[18] 2 Timothy 1:14, 1 Corinthians 4:1

[19] Matthew 11:28-30

[20] Sonny Dean, *Feed Jake*, Pirates of the Mississippi, 1991, Capitol Records Nashville

[21] Grief, https://www.vocabulary.com/dictionary/grief, referenced May 2019

[22] ibid

[23] Mark 15:1-37

[24] John 20:1-18

[25] John 20:19-28

[26] Jesus and Thomas: Doubting Thomas, https://www.trusting-in-jesus.com/jesusandthomas.html, referenced July 25, 2019

[27] St. Thomas Island, https://en.wikipedia.org/wiki/St._Thomas_Island, referenced July 25, 2019

Made in the USA
Columbia, SC
01 September 2019